The Most Wonderful Week of the Year

The Most Wonderful Week of the Year

Roy Berger

Foreword by Bill Mazeroski

BOOKLOGIX®

Alpharetta, Georgia

BOOKLOGIX®
Alpharetta, Georgia

Copyright © 2014 by Roy Berger

Paperback Edition January 2014

ISBN: 978-1-61005-431-7
LCCN: 2013919870

Author e-mail: RoyBerger56@gmail.com

Book website: www.mostwonderfulweek.com

(For information about bulk purchases, please contact the publisher.)

10 9 8 7 6 5 4 3 2   110413

Printed in the United States of America

♾This paper meets the requirements of ANSI/NISO Z39.48-1992 (Permanence of Paper)

For all those kids, like me, who grew up in the 1950s, 60s, and 70s and dreamed about being a major league baseball player but didn't have the talent or ability to make it past Little League. Don't ever let that dream die.

Contents

Foreword

7've played with, against, and watched some great first baseman in all my years in baseball, and I can honestly tell you Roy Berger isn't one of them. However, the enthusiasm for baseball that Roy and these adult fantasy campers show is major league in every way. Pirates Fantasy Camp is one of my favorite weeks of the year. I get to spend time with guys who have now become friends, tell some stories, and what I watch on the field cannot be properly described. You get to see some strange things in the course of a week and have some hearty laughs. I love it.

> – Bill Mazeroski, Pittsburgh Pirates (1956–72)
> 1960 World Series hero.
> 2001 Baseball Hall of Fame Inductee.

Pregame

Prologue

About Fantasy Camp:

"If you think by the way you play today I'm going to sign you, please forget about it."

– Clint Hurdle
Manager, Pittsburgh Pirates.

"One of the important things for people with cancer is to try and do as much as you can for your morale and that defines fantasy baseball camp. I came here never knowing if I would be back again."

– Rev. John Zingaro
six-year fantasy camp veteran.

"I love seeing guys with limited ability break their ass to live that major-league dream."

– Mike Torrez
pitcher, 185-game winner,
1977 World Champion New York Yankees.

"Campers are big-league in every way but one. You know the game, you respect the game, but you don't have the talent of a major leaguer. The heart you have to want to play this game will more than make up for it."

— Jerry "Rolls" Reuss
pitcher, 220 career wins, two-time All-Star.

"I guarantee I had more fun this week than you did."

— Bill Virdon
outfielder, NL Rookie of the Year,
AL & NL Manager of the Year,
1960 World Champion Pittsburgh Pirates.

"Let's take our drubbing and go home."

— Oscar Gamble
outfielder, 200 career home runs,
wore the best Afro in major league history.

"If I have the steal sign on, I will jump in the air and not come back down."

— Mike "Spanky" LaValliere
catcher, Gold Glove Award-winner.

"Start slow and taper off."

— Jim Price
catcher, 1968 World Champion Detroit Tigers.

First Inning

Gathering Dust

*I*t had been over forty years since the last time I competitively slipped it onto my hand, but I knew just where to find it. Once my most prized possession, it had been with me through high school and college graduation, two marriages, two children, a half dozen jobs, and more relocations than I care to remember. It was packed away deep in one of the boxes on a dusty shelf in our garage in the cozy little community with a very high opinion of itself, Mountain Brook, Alabama, just outside of Birmingham.

The box held the miscellany of a twenty-plus-year marriage that I finally got right the second time. It was beneath the surplus of out-of-vogue kitchen gadgets and toys the kids had long since outgrown and forgotten, but I found my childhood baseball glove right away.

The glove, a first baseman's mitt because that's all I ever played, was a gift from my father when I made my very first team, the Dial-A-Car Comets, in 1962. When it was new, it was stiff and reluctant to mold to my hand, but as kids did back in the sixties, I rubbed it over and over with neatsfoot oil, put a baseball in what I wanted to be the pocket, tied some string around it, and then put the glove under my mattress for the winter. Come March, it was soft and ready. Incredibly, all these years later, it still fit perfectly. The webbing was cracked and the leather faded in spots, but it didn't matter to me. It brought back years and years of memories, and I knew a bit of love and attention would be the modern-day cure. After so many years of patiently waiting in the dark and dust, this glove and I were ready to give the best we had left in us.

I remember the first time I put one on. I vaguely remember the last time I took one off.

It was the spring of 1962, and I was an excited ten-year-old. I finally had a real one. No more of those department store varieties with all the team "symbols" on them. Of course, back in those days, we had no idea what a "logo" was.

It was my very first baseball uniform, complete with a dandy matching pair of pants and a hat that helped to authenticate our status as a real baseball team. We might have gotten socks, too. Who can remember?

Now I was a ballplayer. I was a member of the Dial-A-Car Comets of the Central Nassau Athletic Association Little League in East Meadow on Long Island, about twenty-five miles from the center of the baseball universe in New York City.

I still have no idea what Dial-A-Car was. It might have been a limo service or a rental car company. Didn't matter to us ten-year-olds, as they gave us a uniform and a nickname and a baseball-shaped sewn patch that said "Dial-A-Car" right on our chests.

Our hats were emblazoned with a "C" for Comets. It was pretty hip.

There were a dozen of us on the team coached by Armand Lowell, whose son, Abbe, was our second baseman. Abbe decided his future was in law, not baseball, and he now practices on a global stage defending the likes of Bill Clinton and John Edwards. Abbe and I got a lot of playing time on that team. Neither of us was any good, but it helped that his dad was the head coach and mine was the assistant.

The next summer, I played for a team sponsored by Carvel, which was really cool because we didn't care if we won or lost. We just wanted to get the free ice cream after each game. Those two summers wrapped up my Little League career except for the summer of 1964, when I went to Little League baseball camp in Williamsport, Pennsylvania, to develop the skills I really didn't have. And yes—that Williamsport, Pennsylvania—right at the Little League World Headquarters. We played on the showcase field they still use today.

After my early days with the Dial-A-Car and Carvel Ice Cream sponsored teams, I hung up my glove for a few years until 1968. I needed my dad to take up coaching as a profession to have a chance, but he had a family to raise and decided a wholesale seafood business in the Fulton Fish Market would be the ticket to sending three kids to college. By the time I got to high school, I was probably unrealistically feeling confident in my abilities to play baseball. That is, until I realized my misfortune of being unilateral in skill set—first base and only first base—and then I ran into a classmate named Steve Rothenberg.

I hated Steve Rothenberg. He was a starting wide receiver on the Clarke High School (Westbury, New York) football team, starting forward on the basketball team, and a much better first baseman than I was on the baseball team. As sophomores on the Clarke JV team, he played and I watched. I only left the bench to shag a stray foul ball, pick up a thrown bat, or if we were up or down by ten or more runs in the last inning and our coach, Bud Chianese, gave me the pity nod. I got to the plate three times that season—two walks and a strikeout. I'm pretty sure Chianese told me to stand there, don't swing, and see what happened. I'm also certain Rothenberg had the green light at all times.

When that season ended, I took off the uniform for the last time. The Clarke varsity program was good—in fact, very good. The coach, Jack McDonald, told me to not even bother coming out for tryouts. Well, he didn't actually tell me that. Instead, he posted a list of the eighteen guys he wanted as part of the team. My name wasn't on it. Coach McDonald was also a social studies teacher, and I considered going to his office to see if he'd made a mistake. A quick reality check reminded me I rode the pine every game my sophomore year. I watched Steve Rothenberg play first base. Did I mention I hated Steve Rothenberg? I thought better of going to see McDonald and figured if he wanted me, he knew where to find me. As reigning Nassau County "Coach of the Year," he also probably knew what he was doing. After all, he had Rothenberg.

Fate got even with Steve Rothenberg some years later. He became a prosthodontics dentist in Connecticut. But 1969 had been the end of the baseball dream for me. I realized that I would never get paid to play the game professionally. I had no idea that forty-two years later, instead of cashing a check, I could make the dream come true by writing one.

My first team, the 1962 Dial-A-Car Comets. I am middle row left; Dad is back
row right and noted national defense attorney Abbe Lowell is front row center.
That's my brother Mike lingering in the background.

Second Inning

Catching the Late Train

*I*t was February 2009, and I was attending a travel industry trade show. I had been to so many of these events and knew enough people that it made the reheated cocktail food and impersonal hotel staff bearable and occasionally fun at this point in my career. But every now and then, something new and different came up in idle conversation and grabbed a hold of me. On the first night of this conference at the opening cocktail party, I ran into a colleague from New Jersey, Stu Ackerman. Ack was not a guy I was particularly close to, but we'd enjoyed casual banter in the past. I knew Ack, like me, was a devout Yankees fan right down to the branded Yankees credit card he carried in his wallet. We usually swapped stories about the upcoming season, or how bad A-Rod had been last September, but this year surprised me. He couldn't wait to talk about his recent experience at Major League Baseball fantasy camp.

The first time I'd heard of a fantasy camp was about fifteen years earlier in 1993, while living in Wichita, Kansas, and visiting the home of our friends Priscilla and Lou Cohen. Lou, about sixty years old then, was the CEO of a national chain of western wear retail stores based in Wichita. He was a huge Los Angeles Dodgers fan and immediately took me downstairs to see his den. It was a shrine to the Dodgers, and catching your eye right away was the life-sized mannequin dressed in a full Dodgers uniform with the number 21 and "Cohen" inscribed on the back. Lou told me all about his week at Dodgertown in Vero Beach, Florida, three years earlier.

Fantasy baseball camp, unlike its more common namesake fantasy baseball, is a chance for over-the-hill types to put on a uniform and play ball with not only your peers, but also with real major league heroes of yesterday. Fantasy baseball, as we know it today, is a statistical contest of your ability to manage and strategize a team of contemporary players. At fantasy baseball *camp*, you run the risk of getting dirty and probably hurt.

Cohen couldn't stop romanticizing about his experience. He said anyone with a week free and the money to pay for it could go to Florida or Arizona before the "real" players reported for spring training and live their dream of major league stardom. Campers use the team locker rooms, training facilities, and fields. He told me that a good portion of MLB teams ran fantasy camps, and better still, former players coached campers. For a baseball guy like me, it sounded too good to be true.

As we left that night, I told my wife Andi of the conversation in Lou's den and explained the concept of fantasy camp. She asked if it was something I wanted to do. Before I could say "Absolutely!" the reality of raising two kids—then ages thirteen and ten—plus running a business, building a career, and a million other things came crashing down. I nonchalantly said sure, but then forgot about it.

Years later, as Ackerman was telling me about his baseball experience, the enthusiasm returned. I couldn't wait to hear what it was like to be a Yankee for a week. The air left my balloon faster than Maury Wills stealing second when he told me he hadn't been a Yankee after all. Instead, he had just returned from being something called a *Cleveland Indian*.

Ack explained that he'd been asked to go with a couple of friends who were Cleveland fans, and he really had no choice other than the Indians. However, his unbridled enthusiasm made it clear that no matter what uniform he was wearing, it was the experience that took precedence. Even after a full week of being an Indian, he struggled to name any of the ex-players that were in camp, but his memories of the week, the camaraderie, and the laughs put fantasy camp right back at the top of my must-do list.

With my boys out of college and successful in Los Angeles, my business moving in the right direction, and my body beginning to break down and feel every pinch and stretch, I came home and told Andi about Ackerman's Indians experience. She knew about my ongoing passion for baseball and that this would be right up my alley. Incredibly, she hadn't forgotten the 1993 conversation at the Cohens' house in Wichita either. "Let's face it," she said, "the clock is ticking, and you're not getting any younger. I insist you do this next winter." If I'd needed a push, I think I just got shoved.

As a huge Yankees fan, the decision was clear. After a little research, I discovered that because of high demand, the Yankees run camps in November and January, while most other teams run a single January session. Within a week, I received in the mail a classy brochure and DVD of the camp experience. It looked like a blast—a very expensive blast. Over $5K for the week. The list of legends participating in Yankees camps in the past had been impressive. The reality was beginning to form that I might have a chance to play ball with the likes of Chris Chambliss, Bucky Dent, Al Downing, Ken Griffey Sr., Tommy John, Mickey Rivers, Darryl Strawberry, Mike Torrez, and Neil Allen.

Neil Allen? Who on earth is Neil Allen, and how did he crash this party of Yankees legends? I'm not sure Neil Allen is a household name in the Allen household. According to Google, Neil Allen was a Yankee in 1985 and 1987. Career win-loss record through eleven years of getting bounced around the big leagues was 58–70. Was this the stuff fantasy camp is all about? If I am going to play ball with any "Allen," I'd rather throw with my old summer camp chum Joe Allen than toss for the equivalent of a semester's college tuition with Neil Allen.

Disappointed but on a lark, I visited the Pittsburgh Pirates' website to see if they had a fantasy camp. I stared at the computer screen in disbelief—the upcoming 2010 fantasy camp was the fiftieth anniversary of the 1960 World Championship team.

What boy in the late 1950s and 1960s didn't want to grow up to be a major league ballplayer? It was the only sport we followed. The NFL, which had to fight for television exposure, was a winter diversion until spring training. The NBA was a novelty act and had to play weekend doubleheaders with four teams in one city to get anyone to notice. Every shot was worth two points, and nobody had ever heard of a "slam dunk." The league's winningest player, Bill Russell, was a defensive specialist. Boring. Hockey was played in four eastern US cities: New York, Chicago, Boston, and Detroit. No Americans played in the NHL, which made it very tough to garner interest or for kids to aspire to play.

Baseball truly was the singular American game and national pastime. In New York, everyone had been spoiled with three teams to root for until 1958, when the New York Giants and Brooklyn Dodgers caught a train out West. Then, for four long years, National League fans with loyalty to the Dodgers or Giants waited until the next morning to learn how their favorites did as West Coast games began back East at ten p.m. Some lost interest, but none became Yankees fans—they were too despicable in the mind of a Dodgers or Giants fan to ever be able to root for. Finally, in 1962, baseball gave New York back the National League (well, sort of) with a team called the New York Metropolitans.

The Mets were awful. This made it fun if you were a Yankees fan and didn't want to be bothered with mediocrity. It was painful to be a charter Mets fan, but after a while and after losing 100 games their very first season, they became a bit of a parody of themselves. Eventually everyone became a Mets fan in their very own way. The start-up die-hard Mets fans suffered through all the misery on the field, while the Dodgers, Giants, and Yankees backers looked on with a strange mixture of amusement and pity at their ineptness.

I was neither a Yankees nor Mets fan. I hated the Yankees, and like everyone else in 1962, I felt sorry for the Mets. The Pittsburgh Pirates were my team. I was probably the only Pirates fan in East Meadow, New York. Actually, I was one of probably only two Pirates fans in our little Long Island town. The other one was my dad. As they say down South, "I got it honest."

My father, Herb Berger, was born in the shadows of Yankee Stadium in the Bronx in 1928. By rights, he should have been a Yankees or New York Giants fan, but he wasn't. The first love of his life was the Pittsburgh Pirates, and it remained that way until 1949 when he married a cute gal with auburn hair a year his junior. Arlene Sachs, my mother, stole his heart and became his wife. Baseball took a backseat to married life.

While perhaps becoming relegated to second fiddle, the Pirates were always my dad's team. Back in the 1930s he liked a pair of brothers who played for the Bucs—Paul and Lloyd Waner. Dad grew up in Washington Heights on 189th Street about forty blocks from the Giants' home, the Polo Grounds, which was easily accessible by a two-mile walk, or if you had a spare nickel, you could ride the trolley right to the ballpark.

At every opportunity, he would go see the Pirates when they came to town. For twenty-five cents, you could get a nice seat in the bleachers and take all the abuse you could handle from the Giants fans whose teams were always better than the lowly Buccaneers. Fortunately, my dad didn't have to suffer the guff alone since his high school classmate, Andy Economedis, was also a Pirates fan. They had each other's shoulders to cry on.

The Pirates virus led my father to become a Pittsburgh sports fan. To this day, he pulls for the Steelers and can even remember when Pittsburgh had a professional basketball team for a season in 1946–47, the Ironmen. Stranger than being a Pirates fan in upper Manhattan is the fact that Dad has never been to Pittsburgh. Never. Go figure.

It was natural, or "honest," that I became a Pirates fan. If it was good enough for Dad, it was good enough for me. You are always influenced by your idols. My earliest baseball memory is of the 1960 Pittsburgh Pirates. I can still recite by memory the starting lineup from that team: Hoak, Groat, Mazeroski, Stuart, Skinner,

Virdon, Clemente, Burgess, and the starting pitching rotation of Friend, Law, Haddix, and Mizell. Amazing how some things stick with you through time, yet what happened thirty minutes ago can fade away.

The 1960 World Series was when the Pirates beat the brash Yankees four games to three, despite being outscored in the seven-game set 55–27. It was arguably the most lopsided seven-game World Series in baseball history. The three games the Yankees won were by the scores of 16–3, 10–0, and 12–0. The Pirates won 6–4, 3–2, 5–2, and 10–9. It's funny how you can be deceived by your memory sometimes. After going back and reading about the 1960 World Series and watching a DVD of the classic, I realized I remember virtually nothing about the first six games other than what history had preserved.

Game 7 on October 13, 1960, for all the baseball marbles was a different story. It was a Thursday and a school day. Then the World Series games were played during the day, and while all were televised, not many folks had access to a television set during work and school. However, everyone had something called a transistor radio, a pocket-sized machine about the size of a pack of cigarettes of incredible virtue that one used either to listen to Chubby Checker or the World Series, most of the time in a covert manner. All transistors came with this snappy little headphone that you could plug into your ear so no one else could hear it.

I was eight years old and in the third grade at Meadowbrook Elementary School. I'm not sure whether my parents gave me permission or if I just snuck the radio on the school bus with me that morning. It didn't matter; it was Game 7, and my Pirates were going to win. I just knew it. I had to listen.

Coincidentally, that afternoon during school I had to visit the restroom many times. One of those times I told my teacher, Miss Reich, I thought I drank too much milk at lunch. I told her I couldn't help myself. The clandestine transistor radio always came with me. The Pirates at Pittsburgh's Forbes Field jumped out to a 4–0 lead behind Vernon Law in the second inning only to see the Yankees chip away and take a 7–4 advantage to the bottom of the eighth with about twenty minutes remaining until the school bell rang. I missed the Pirates rally for five runs in the eighth behind backup catcher Hal Smith's three-run homer to go ahead 9–7, and only three outs away from being World Champions.

I was on the school bus heading home when the Yankees got two in the ninth off starter-turned-seventh-game-reliever Bob Friend to tie the game. I bolted through the front door of 90 Leona Court, ran downstairs, and turned on the Admiral TV set just in time to see Ralph Terry throw a fastball to Bill Mazeroski that was high and away for a ball. The next pitch is a moment forever etched in my mind, Pittsburghers', and baseball history. Maz sent the baseball 406 feet over the left field wall as Yogi Berra could just turn and look for the first ever World Series deciding walk-off home run and a championship for my Pirates!

I was wearing my black Pirates replica batting helmet with gold lettering, and I sprinted outside and starting emulating Maz running around the bases before Yogi had time to utter the immortal words, "We made too many wrong mistakes to win." In Brooklyn, thirteen-year-old Larry David, a huge Yankees fan, admittedly sat and cried—a dozen years before making people laugh for a living. Mickey Mantle, twenty-eight, openly wept while taking off the pinstripes in the Yankees locker room.

14

Meanwhile, to the victors go the spoils as I pranced and waved my helmet with unbridled joy.

Dad was working at his Uncle Al's belt and pocketbook factory, Debutant, at Thirty-Second Street and Fifth Avenue in New York. Normally he left the shop at three p.m., caught the three-thirty Long Island Rail Road to Hicksville, and would be through our front door at four thirty p.m.

I sat in the living room and stared out the big bay window. It was now four thirty, and I could always count on Dad to pull into our Long Island driveway promptly at four thirty p.m. Not this day, however. As he was walking to Penn Station, transistor radio in his ear, the Yankees were in the process of tying the game in the ninth so he diverted to E. J. Korvette's, the first of the big box discount retail stores of the era. Korvette's was on Thirty-Fourth Street, only a few blocks from the train station, but the train could wait for the seventh game to conclude. Masses of people lined up in front of the storefront to watch the TV picture through the glass showcase window. At 3:36 p.m., thirty-two years of frustration became worth the wait. As the Pirates celebrated, Dad threw his hands in the air and yelled, "Finally!" as the Yankees fans scurried away in a hurry, while the rest of New York hustled to get home and settle in front of their Philco or Westinghouse or RCA TV sets—some even had color—to watch the third Kennedy-Nixon presidential debate that night.

I paced; my heart was racing, and I didn't know how much longer I could contain it. Five o'clock came, and the sun began to disappear on this gorgeous fall day.

"Ma, where is he?" I yelled into the kitchen. "Where's Dad, and when is he coming home?"

With her hands full between cooking dinner and minding my little brothers—Mike, a whiny five-year-old, and Kenny, who alternated between sleeping and crying as seven-month-olds are wont to do—my mother shouted back, "He probably caught a later train, dear. He'll be home soon."

Finally at five thirty, headlights approached, and I could see it was Dad's black 1956 Hudson Hornet. With sheer excitement, I bolted through the screen door. Before my father had a chance to close the car door, I grabbed him and gave him a huge hug. "We did it! I can't believe we won!" I shouted to anyone listening within miles. Dad gave me a great big smile and smothering hug and knocked the Pirates helmet right off my head.

October 13, 1960, was the best day of this eight-year-old's life. Dad and I were World Champions!

My affinity for the Pirates remained strong through the 1960s. As the nights got deeper and the old AM radio signals got clearer, I couldn't wait to pretend to be asleep only to hear Bob Prince call the Pirates game on KDKA radio in Pittsburgh. Talk about radio technology. In those days, you could get a Pittsburgh radio station (only at night) in New York. That was even better than the transistor radio. What would they think of next?

The radio was one of those boxy types at my headboard. I didn't think you could ever get more excited in bed than listening to a Pirates game (it took a few more years for me to figure out that fallacy). I had no idea what Iron City Beer was, and I couldn't wait for my first one, but if it was good enough for my heroes to drink, it was good enough for me. I used to take every Pirates loss hard. There was nothing sweeter than to hear Prince with raised voice after every Pirates win cry, "We had 'em all the way!" I never slept as soundly as I did after a Pirates victory.

I couldn't believe it, the 1960 World Series-winning Pirates. For an entire week, my earliest and most precious childhood sports memory could come alive. I told Andi, "I think this is it! I think I'm going to do it."

"Yankees camp?" she asked.

"Nope," I said, "Pittsburgh Pirates." After more than two decades of watching me cheer the New York Yankees, I'm not sure she understood. I don't expect many would. But the eight-year-old boy in me was leaping with joy once again.

There was only one shot at this for a fiftieth anniversary celebration: January 17–24, 2010, in Bradenton, Florida. The cost was a bit more digestible at $3,750. Yankees camp would always be there. So, too, might Neil Allen.

Kent Tekulve, former great Pirates relief pitcher, was the fantasy camp director. Joe Billetdeaux, the camp coordinator. Among the legends taking part in camp were my 1960 idols Bob Friend, Vernon Law, Joe Gibbon, Bob Skinner, Bob Oldis, Bill Virdon, and of course, Bill Mazeroski. These guys had always been larger than life to me, and the prospect of shaking their hands, let alone playing ball with them, filled me with equal measures of delight and trepidation.

The seven heroes from 1960, in their twenties and so youthful fifty years before, were now mid to late seventies in age. Clearly the list of surviving and healthy ballplayers from fifty years ago was dwindling. To round out the camp coaching roster of sixteen for the week were some of the more contemporary Pirates like Steve Blass, Dave Cash, and Rennie Stennett from the 1971 World Series championship team, along with Sid Bream, Mike LaValliere, Zane Smith, Grant Jackson, and Jerry Reuss. Player-turned-broadcaster John Wehner would also be in attendance. For the Pirates, it was a pretty impressive list.

Before I enrolled I got in touch with Billetdeaux to learn more about the demographics of the typical camper. I had no interest in spending a full week being pushed around by a bunch of twenty-five-year-olds, nor did I want the teams to be fielded principally by octogenarians.

He told me there would be about seventy-five to eighty campers ranging in age from thirty to the early seventies. The average camper's age was mid-fifties. I told him that I didn't want to embarrass myself. He told me I would fit right in. I'm still not sure if that answer was a good one or not.

The next step was to see if I could still hit a baseball. My throwing had become a struggle over the years, but if I couldn't come close to seeing or hitting the ball, I was staying home. There was no point in tormenting myself. I had no idea how fast some of these guys could pitch, and though I hoped I would be facing more seventy-year-old campers than thirty-year-old ones, I didn't want to set myself up for humiliation and failure.

I found an indoor batting range about fifteen minutes from home and set the speed at sixty to seventy mph. I made contact with the ball.

I sent the Pirates a check.

Dad still sports his Pirates cap.

1960 WORLD SERIES

GAME #7

Mazeroski's Homer Wins It!

My favorite baseball card ever.

Third Inning

Honoring Heroes

January 2010

Sunday

*T*oday's the day. My bags are packed. The glove and shoes are accounted for. My boarding pass is printed. The idea of staying in bed and putting this fantasy to rest really does have some appeal.

My flight to Tampa leaves at noon. Once I land, I plan to drive south for about an hour to Bradenton. I've rented a car for the week rather than take the camp shuttle, so I can pick up and leave Pirate City if I need some baseball-free sanity time. An added benefit is I have the ability to head back to the airport and escape early if things don't go very well.

We are to report to the dorm at Pirate City by five p.m. The evening welcome reception begins an hour later. Just in case I come to my senses, I have a reservation booked on a Southwest flight back to Birmingham that leaves at eight p.m. No kidding.

Despite the 1960 Pittsburgh Pirates being my earliest childhood sports memory, I was still only eight when they beat the Yankees in the World Series, and so much of it has faded with time. Over the past few months, I've read as much as I could about the team, and in particular, the "legends" who are going to be at this fantasy camp. In my memory, only the victorious Game 7 lives on, so I got up to speed on the other six games of the series that were played before Mazeroski's home run caused me to dance a jig on my front lawn.

It was all great stuff that I devoured in rehashing. I read up on the individual accomplishments of the seven guys from that team who will be at camp. These guys played baseball because they loved the game. In 1960 a very good salary was $15,000 for the season, and most of the players worked a second job during the off-season to help pay bills. The winning 1960 World Series share per player was $8,400; the Yankees got $5,200 each for losing. By comparison, the 2009 World Champion Yankees got $365,000 each, while the Phillies took home $265,000 for a losing effort. Probably takes the sting out of losing just a little bit.

Reading about and watching the 1960 Pirates highlights were a lot easier than training for this week at camp. It had been years since I'd put on a glove. After a few years of Little League and a disheartening stint on my high school JV baseball squad, my first baseman's mitt only saw the light of day on the softball fields during collegiate intramurals or in the local beer leagues. I did the obligatory coaching of my kids' Little League teams too, and by the time they outgrew it, I thought I had as well, but subconsciously I was longing for more.

I have always been a first baseman. Growing up, I had the perfect credentials for the position: tall, lanky, left-handed, and extremely slow. When the Pirates sent the initial camp questionnaire, I was asked for my three preferences of position. My first choice was first base. My second choice was first base. My third choice was first base. And in case there was any misunderstanding, I wrote in a fourth choice: first base.

Fortunately, my son Jason had some free time over the holidays in December, and we did quite a bit of throwing—first in Birmingham and then on a field in South Florida. I actually threw a bit better than I thought I would, considering I hadn't thrown a ball in some twenty-five years.

I could still catch, but the almost-fifty-year-old first baseman's glove didn't last very long as one of Jason's tosses tore right through the webbing. We found a shoemaker who stitched it back up for $7. I hope it holds for the week.

While playing catch with Jason, I became conscious of how the years have caught up with me. I could still catch the ball, but I had no flexibility at all. If the ball was to the left or right, it went past me. I could probably get in front of a ground ball, but wasn't sure I could get back up. As far as throwing goes, let's just say that if it's important enough for the runner to go from second to third on a putout at first base, well, he's got it.

For a month and a half leading up to camp, I rented a batting cage for half an hour once a week. The pitch speed was set at about seventy mph, which got past me before I saw it. I doubt we'll see pitching that fast on a regular basis at camp. At least, I hope not. But I've been hanging in, and I know that at the minimum, I'll have some timing when I face the live pitches. I've been using aluminum bats at the cages, and we'll use wood at camp. One clean base hit will make my week. I think I'm prepared, but who knows?

This will actually be my third visit to Bradenton, and unfortunately, neither of the other two were an invitation to participate in the famed Nick Bollettieri Tennis Academy located a few miles from Pirate City. The first was in 1972 when I was a sophomore across Alligator Alley at the University of Miami. I headed out to Pirates spring training with my college pal Jim Skonieczny. We called him "Scratch" because nobody could pronounce Skonieczny. Scratch was from Pittsburgh and just as crazy about the Pirates as I was. We took a Trailways bus from Miami and five hours later arrived at the Pirates spring training site. The Pirates were coming off the 1971 World Championship title having beaten Baltimore in seven games just five months earlier.

I'll admit that in 1972 at the age of twenty, some of the luster of the ballplayer idol worship had worn off. I wasn't the starry-eyed kid I had been back in the early sixties, but it was still worth the bus trip and a lot of fun to watch the players scrimmage for a day. I even got to take a picture with my favorite player ever: Hall of Famer Roberto Clemente. In those innocent days, he was strolling alone from field to field, and I walked over and asked if he wouldn't mind posing for a picture with me. He couldn't have been nicer.

Scratch took the picture. I couldn't believe I had a picture of me and Clemente. Of course, we had to wait until we got back to Miami to have the film developed. Then it took another three or four days to be processed. I remember racing to the bookstore at The U to get the pictures. And there it was—a great shot of me and half of someone's body and his right arm. My one shot forever with my ballplayer idol. Roberto and me, immortalized with me in a picture of someone's right arm. Tragically, Mr. Clemente died nine months later. Needless to say, Scratch didn't go into a career in photojournalism.

My second visit to Bradenton was a few weeks before camp on Christmas Eve day. Jason and I were driving south from Orlando to spend some time with my parents at Del Boca Vista. We diverted to Bradenton because I wanted to take a look at the setup before I arrived for camp the following month.

We were greeted and escorted by Rachelle Madrigal, who works in the sales department at Pirate City. She was extremely gracious and showed us the entire complex. It was all very impressive, from the private and public areas, to the dormitory rooms, to the lounges, to the dining room and the spic-and-span clubhouse.

Pirate City is a beautiful complex on a very hard-to-find tract of land and far nicer than the major league product the Pirates put on the field. Recently renovated in 2008 to the tune of $20 million, there are four main areas on the footprint. The headquarters building is an eighty-three-room dormitory used year-round, mainly for minor leaguers either training or rehabbing, though the big-league Pirates are here from February through late March. It was money well spent, and it created a much more impressive facility than you would expect from a team that has not had a winning season in seventeen years. Surrounding the main building is a cafeteria to the front, the gorgeous clubhouse, locker room and training facility to the rear, and then four regulation-sized playing fields out back. It was a bit intimidating to walk onto the ball fields and think about performing on the same field the pros use, but I was glad to get a taste prior to camp and that I was able to share the moment with my oldest son.

Now, I'm headed back to Bradenton for the third time, and this time it's for real. I received the attendee list early last week. There are sixteen ex-major leaguers to guide the eighty-three campers through the week. Campers range in age from thirty (the minimum age allowed) to seventy-seven. There are four campers in their seventies, and the average age is fifty-four. I already hate the thirty-year-olds. Understandably, approximately half of the roster is from Pennsylvania, but the rest are coming in from fourteen other states and Canada. Later, I discovered that one player traveled for sixteen hours from an outpost called Anderson, Alaska. When Scotty Ray left home, it was thirty degrees below zero. Bradenton was eighty-two degrees on his arrival. He left his jacket on the bus.

Each room in the Pirate City dorm is named after a Pirate great from years past (yes, there were some) with pictures and memorabilia on the walls. Almost all campers are housed in the dorm. I had time to freshen up and then headed over to the opening banquet in the adjacent dining hall, which was gussied up with a couple of bars and video screens for the banquet. It became obvious pretty quickly that most of the campers had been here before, and the dinner had the lighthearted feel of a reunion.

Before sitting down, I roamed the room and tried to put names with faces of the ballplayers, especially my 1960 guys. Then the moment got surreal. Very surreal. About fifteen feet away from me was Bill Mazeroski. He had a few more pounds, less hair, and a few more facial lines. Even though fifty years had passed, for a fleeting minute it was 1960 again. Normally I'm not at a loss for words, but I froze, and as much as I wanted to go over and say hello, introduce myself, and thank him for a lifetime of memories for me and my dad, I just couldn't.

I felt dizzy and very unprepared for my reaction to seeing idols standing in front of me. I had the same reaction with Bill Virdon, who looks just like he did from his playing and managing days. Vern Law was easily recognizable. Put some hair back and take a few pounds off Bob Friend and his image comes right back. Bob Skinner was tall and lanky, and once he was pointed out to me, he too came back as clear as the 1960 World Championship. I had no chance of recognizing Bob Oldis and Joe Gibbon, not because their looks may have changed, but they were little-used and not in my kid scope back in the sixties.

I shook my head back to reality and sat down with three other camp rookies. Two of them had given the camp to themselves as a twenty-fifth wedding anniversary gift. No kidding. Their wives wanted diamonds, and they wanted to go to Pirates camp. The third "rookie" was celebrating his fiftieth birthday. We made idle chatter as the returning campers told old camp stories and shared memories of past experiences.

A tall, distinguished gent walked by our table and asked to join us. Even though it had been years since I'd seen him play, I recognized Jerry Reuss in an instant. He'd won 220 games with eight teams over the course of his career and was a two-time all-star. He ended his career as a Pirate in 1990. Only at a fantasy baseball camp would a former major leaguer with over two hundred career wins ask to join four baseball rubes for dinner.

Camp director and former major league reliever Tekulve, sixty-three and still wearing intimidating glasses, went over the rules and regs for the week and then introduced the sixteen major leaguers who would be our coaches, saving the seven members of the championship 1960 Pirates for last. Bill Mazeroski—the reason all of us Pirates fans were here this week—got a standing ovation. It was the fifteenth consecutive camp that Maz had graced with his presence, wit, and respect for everyone else in the room.

Someone at our table asked Reuss, sixty, what we rooks could expect this week.

"Campers are big-league in every way but one," he said. "You know the game, you respect the game, but you don't have the talent of a major leaguer. The heart you have to want to play this game will more than make up for it. You'll hear a lot of baseball stories, most of which we hope you forget by the time you go home. And you'll have more fun this week than you could ever imagine."

I called Southwest and canceled my flight.

We report to the clubhouse tomorrow morning at eight o'clock.

Monday

I arrived at the cafeteria when it opened at seven fifteen the next morning. The guy in front of me was toting a bag seemingly filled with baseball bats. He wasn't the only one. There was bat bag upon bat bag and duffels filled to the brim with player equipment. The cafeteria floor looked like the tarmac at an airport while a major league team prepared to board the flight.

I was either surrounded by serious ballplayers or megalomaniacs. All I'd brought with me—two fielding gloves, two batting gloves, an undershirt, shorts, and a pair of twenty-dollar Nike baseball shoes from Dick's—was crammed into a plastic Westin Hotel laundry bag with "Fresh Laundry" inscribed on the side. I ate breakfast with the bag carefully hidden under my chair.

At 8:05 a.m., the procession to the clubhouse began. We looked like a marching band as all eighty-three campers stepped in tandem with the pro staff for the clubhouse unveiling. So much of baseball life and sanctity is spent in the clubhouse. Now we really become major leaguers.

It was beautiful. The real Pirates use this clubhouse during their spring training, set to start in three weeks, and the fact that I'm using it first this season leaves me giddy and a bit humbled. It feels well worth the money already to see my name engraved on a nameplate above my handsome, oak-finished locker. Two uniforms with my name and number are hanging in place. We have a home white and an away black uniform along with a nice practice jersey, white pants, black socks, and two hats.

We all had our choice of uniform number for the week. The natural choice for me was #21 for my baseball hero, Roberto Clemente, but I thought that was too hokey. There are nine in camp this week who took #21. Bill Mazeroski, #9, would have been my next pick; there are twelve campers wearing #9.

My first base idols for the Pirates growing up, Donn Clendenon (#17) and Willie Stargell (#8), are both deceased, and I just had to let them rest in peace and not butcher their positions. Thus, I chose #56 for a guy born on May 6.

We got dressed, figured out how to put on the socks and belts, and eighty-three Pirates, all in home white uniforms, met on the ball field for our opening day orders.

Each morning there will be "recognition awards" before we begin our games. The recognition awards are actually a "kangaroo court" presided over by Camp Commissioner Steve Blass. Steve, sixty-six, is an ex-great Pirate pitcher and 1971 World Champion who does television and radio broadcasts of the home games. He's also a funny guy.

Kangaroo court is a longtime baseball clubhouse staple. Though my own baseball career was limited, all baseball fans know of this tradition in which trumped-up charges are made against players for infractions large and small and restitution meted out. Here at Pirates camp, Blass is a one-man court—judge and jury—and he levies fines for transgressions from the previous day. All fines are to be paid and are donated to The Boys and Girls Club of Manatee County, home county of Bradenton.

We gathered on the right field grass of one of the Pirate City fields, and Blass asked for a show of hands from everyone who called home last night. About twenty-five hands were raised, including mine. Blass said, "That's a $1 fine. You are here this week for baseball and booze and not to be calling home." He then asked for a show of hands for everyone who didn't call home last night. Fifty hands went into the air. Blass said, "That's a $2 fine for not giving a shit about what's going on at home."

Stretching followed and then the real deal. We were split into eight teams for an evaluation game. Seven innings and the score irrelevant, but the pros were watching. The pros will serve as our coaches, and each one needed to gain a sense of our abilities before they draft their teams for league play. The umpires all week are NCAA college baseball types of various levels. The officiating is sure to be much better than the caliber of play.

I was put on Team 2 for the evaluation contest. We were the visiting team. We batted in alphabetical order, so guess who became the camp leadoff batter?

I haven't had butterflies in a long time, but as I stepped into the batter's box for the first time in a "real" ball game since 1968, I could feel some fluttering. I wasn't really nervous, more apprehensive about something I haven't done in forever, and I didn't know that I was capable. All I kept thinking was, *Just get this over with.*

It's funny how sometimes old and long-forgotten habits return. In the mid to late seventies I was a fairly decent tennis player. In 1977, I was ranked in the upper end of the top 100 twenty-five-year-old male tennis players in the state of Florida for one ranking period, which lasts about three months. In those days, whenever I served the tennis ball, I would touch the top of each sock before serving. No idea why, just a little tick. So when I walked up to the plate for the first time and got ready to hit with a million thoughts racing through my mind, what's the first thing I catch myself doing? Yep, the socks.

My first time up was a two pitch at-bat with pitches considerably slower than I'd faced at the batting cage at home. I grounded a ball past the pitcher that was fielded by the shortstop over second base. In a bang-bang play at first, he threw me out by about fifteen steps. I was going to ask for a replay but had a feeling it was a good call. As I huffed toward first, I kept thinking what a schlep it was to get there.

In the bottom of the first, as I stood at first base on defense, I heard behind me, "Hey, Alabama, how you doing?" It was Mazeroski with a camp roster in hand. In all my eight-year-old fantasies about Bill Mazeroski, I never imagined that one day he would notice me, or that the kid from New York would ever be referred to as "Alabama." And thankfully, he had more guts to approach me than I did last night when I first saw him and froze. Talk about a big-league welcome. Wow. I was awestruck and stood there with a smile as wide as the Monongahela River!

Things continued to get better. I walked on a 3–2 pitch my second time up and then got two base hits in my final two at-bats. The first was a ground shot into left field, and the second one may be the best ball I'd hit all week. A 3–2 line drive solidly hit over the second baseman into right field. I've gotta tell you—it was a thrill and felt really good.

The problem was I had to run the bases. My first two times on base were with two outs, so the inning ended soon after. My final hit was with one out, and the next guy singled to left as I lumbered to second. *Why are those damn bases so far apart?*

The next batter hits what I think is a double play ball to short as I chug to third. I told the third baseman, "I'm so winded right now it's going to take a double to score me." They proceeded to botch the DP, leaving me safe at third.

I actually scored a run when a ground ball, which should have ended the inning, was dropped at first and allowed me to get home and catch my breath. All those weeks I spent playing catch with Jason and hitting the batting cages, I guess I should have been on the field jogging as well.

All in all, it was a good start. I was 2–3 with a walk and a run scored. I played six innings in the field and did not record one putout, a baseball rarity for a first baseman. I think we won the game, but nobody kept score and nobody cared. It was very cordial and a real fun time to be doing something that I have not done for many years. I also was relieved to see the pitching by and large was in the neighborhood of fifty to fifty-five mph. At that level, I knew I could compete.

I hustled back to my room and before even taking a shower I couldn't wait to call my dad to tell him about my first day in a real Pirates uniform. It didn't matter that I was fifty-seven and he was eighty. What mattered was we were still together and could talk about an experience that neither one of us ever saw coming. For a few minutes, once again it was five thirty p.m. on October 13, 1960, on our Long Island driveway.

Tuesday

Yesterday, the line at eight a.m. stretched from the cafeteria to the door as eighty-three campers and sixteen staff made the very tough decision of whether or not they wanted bacon with their eggs. This morning, the line was different. Everyone rushed to the clubhouse to see the team selections, who was on which team, and managed and coached by whom.

I got to the clubhouse a couple of minutes before eight and found out that based on Monday's evaluation game I was put on the "Wagners" (all teams are named after former Pirate greats); my manager would be Bill Virdon, assisted by my dinner companion, Jerry Reuss.

It was pretty neat to think of being managed for the week by Virdon. He was originally signed by the Yankees in 1950, spent a couple of springs in Yankees training camp, and quickly realized he was never going to be the Yankees center fielder as long as #7 was patrolling the territory. He was traded away from Mickey

Mantle to St. Louis in 1954 and in 1955 became the National League Rookie of the Year.

Bill played eleven seasons in the big leagues, from 1955 to 1965, and then again for a year in 1968. He won the National League Rookie of the Year award with St. Louis in 1955. The Pirates rewrote franchise history in 1956 when Pittsburgh shipped Bobby Del Greco and Dick Littlefield to the Cardinals for Virdon.

He played a key role in the 1960 World Series win over the Yankees with ESPN-worthy Play of the Day highlights, nineteen years before there was an ESPN. He made what proved to be crucial catches in Game 1 off the bat of Yogi Berra and Game 4 off Bob Cerv. However, one of the most famous plays in World Series history began with Virdon in the eighth inning of Game 7.

With Gino Cimoli on first, the Pirates trailing, and opportunity running out, Virdon hit a ground ball to shortstop Tony Kubek that had double play written all over it. The ball hit a rock, then hit Kubek in the throat, felling the Yankee and keeping the rally alive as the Pirates went on to score five runs to take the lead. Though the Yankees tied the game in the top of the ninth, it still paved the way for the Mazeroski World Series walk-off.

I asked Virdon what he was thinking when he hit the ground ball to Kubek. "Oh shit!" was my skipper's answer.

Bill spent the next nine years in center field for the Pirates compiling a .267 career batting average and won a Gold Glove in 1962. Despite being seventy-eight years old at fantasy camp, he still looked tough as a saddle and easily could have been cast as an extra in a John Wayne movie. He just had that look about him.

Virdon also knows how to fill out a lineup card. Before ever imagining he would be leading Roy Berger in fantasy camp, he managed in the majors for twelve years from 1972 to 1984 with the Pirates, Yankees, Astros, and Expos. He won two division titles in his managerial career: 1972 with Pittsburgh and 1980 in Houston. He compiled a 995–921 record for a winning percentage of .519 and was Manager of the Year in the American League with the Yankees in 1974 and in the National League with Houston in 1980.

He is also the answer to one of baseball's great trivia questions: which full-time Yankees manager never managed a game in Yankee Stadium? During Virdon's years with the Yankees, 1974–75, the stadium was undergoing renovations, and the Yankees played their home games for two years in the Mets park at Shea Stadium.

The hometown rival's digs didn't have the majesty of the stadium in the Bronx, but the neighborhood didn't bother Virdon as he lead the Yankees to a 89–73 record in 1974, good enough for second place in the American League and Manager of the Year.

Yankee Stadium wasn't ready for the 1975 season either, and the Yankees stumbled a bit, which was enough for George Steinbrenner to pull the plug on Virdon's tenure in New York and replace him with Billy Martin on August 1. The Yankees were 53–51 at the time, but it was no secret Steinbrenner never wanted Virdon in the first place (he wanted to hire Dick Williams), and when Martin became available for the first of many stints with the Yankees, Virdon became expendable. You won't meet a finer gentleman than Bill Virdon.

"Quail," as Virdon is known to his contemporaries for his dying quail style base hits that always seemed to find a spot to fall safely in the outfield, had shaken off the firing by the time we took the field thirty-five years later.

Our assistant coach, Reuss, pitched for twenty-one years with 220 career wins, over 1,900 strikeouts, a 3.64 lifetime ERA, and a no-hitter as a Dodger in 1980 against the Giants. He was intimidating as a 6'5" tall, blond, left-handed hurler. He was nicknamed "Rolls" by ESPN's Chris Berman and the name stuck.

Even if our team isn't good, we certainly have experience and smarts managing us.

Before today's games, we again assembled on the outfield grass for the Blass kangaroo court. First fine of the day for $1 was to a player wearing a Steelers sweatshirt at Pirates camp. I immediately put my glove over the "NY" on my jacket, as all I have with me is a Yankees warm-up coat.

Other fines of note were $10 to a camper who smoked ten cigarettes during Monday's evaluation game, and another $10 to the camper who went to a Tampa strip club the night before and only brought a bottle of water back for Blass. Blass made it perfectly clear: if you are going to a strip club and you want to bring him something back, a bottle of water falls far short of his expectations.

Largest fine of the day was for the camper who called Steve Blass "Bill Blass" the day before. Steve told him that Bill Blass was gay and dead. The camper shot back, "It's easy to see how I got confused." He was fined a record $250.

After our morning stretch, it was time to start league play. Game rules are close to the real deal. There is no bunting or stealing, but everything else is fair. We play a full seven innings with campers pitching the whole time and no "run rule" to end games early. Play until you're finished. Though no stealing is allowed, the average speed of just about all of the campers is so slow that you are allowed to lead off the bases to the infield cut out. It also helps not getting tossed out at second on a teammate's clean base hit. That wouldn't be looked upon too favorably by the guy who gets the hit.

Our first opponents were the "Waners," managed by John Wehner and assisted by Rennie Stennett.

Our starting pitcher, David Briles, is the forty-year-old son of the late Pirate pitcher Nelson Briles. Nellie won 129 games in the majors and passed away way too soon at the age of sixty-one in 2005. His legacy continues every January at Pirate City, as Nellie was the innovator behind the Pirates fantasy camp fifteen years ago. David, who lives in Columbus, Ohio, is a very nice young man, and he would make his dad proud.

David gave us three strong innings. Immediately, I noticed how much more serious and competitive everyone was compared to the evaluation games. Virdon penciled me in the lineup at first base and batting sixth, probably both spots justifiable based upon the Monday practice game. I was just excited to be put into a lineup by Bill Virdon.

In my first at-bat, I lined a shot into right field for a single. The hit was solid and in that at-bat, I accomplished my goal for the week—a solid base hit in a game that counted. I got what I paid for, there were still four days left, and anything else from this point forward was a bonus.

As our inning ended, I trotted back out to first base for the bottom of the second, and the first base coach for the Waners said, "Way to see the ball, Berger; nice hit." That came from Stennett, former Pirate second baseman from 1971 to 1979, lifetime .274 hitter, and the only player in major league history to go seven for seven in a nine-inning game. He's telling me, a sore fifty-seven-year-old who can hardly walk, "nice hit"? Is this a great game or what?

My second at-bat produced a ground ball toward short that the shortstop couldn't come up with and pushed our first run across the plate. The official scorer, sensing I was shorted gifts for Hanukkah, gave me a hit and an RBI, and we took the lead for good. My third time up, I walked.

I had a good game in the field as well. Seven or eight putouts, a scoop putout in the second inning, and a pop-up that I trapped against my chest before I had an opportunity to call a fair catch. Coupled with my 2–2 day at the plate and an RBI, I exceeded my goals in one fell swoop.

We ended the game on a 6–4–3 double play that clinched the 4–0 blanking and then quickly squeezed in lunch with our second game scheduled to start about ninety minutes later. Lunchtime conversation taught me how rare a camp shutout win is.

We played the "Vaughans" in the afternoon game, managed by Pirates 1960 outfielder Bob Skinner and assisted by pitcher Zane Smith.

It wasn't much of a contest as we won 16–7 with fifty-four-year-old former Pittsburgh police officer Kevin Kubala on the mound. I was a tired 1–4 and a walk with a lineout to third—a feel-good, windblown shot over the right fielder's head for a single and two RBIs (no matter how far that ball went past the right fielder, it was only going to be a single for me; second base was too far away). I walked my third time up and grounded to second my fourth time at-bat.

My final time up, I faced Scott May—son of former Pirate catcher Milt May—who was on the Pirates spring training instructional staff. The Vaughans ran out of pitchers, and we agreed to let Scott pitch since we had a nine-run lead. May brought heat compared to the campers, and I was lucky to foul off a couple of pitches. I finally got called out on a fastball around my ankles. I was tempted to turn to the ump and say, "This may be fantasy camp, but you don't have to call fantasy strikes," but at 16–7, I left it to save my arguing for another day.

As a team, we had an acceptable defensive day, including another 6–4–3 double play that caught the attention of the Pirate TV crew for the camp DVD. A doubleheader sweep is a nice way to start league play.

By the end of the day, we are tired, weary, and sore. Mercifully, there will be only one game tomorrow. We play at eleven a.m. at McKechnie Field, the spring home stadium of the Pirates.

Campers stayed late into the night in the World Series Lounge, located on the third floor of the Pirate City dorm, drinking and carousing and generally getting to know one another. I went for a while, stood outside on the veranda, and enjoyed a glass of red wine and a cigar to celebrate the combination of our two victories and the fact I got through the day. Maz, cigar at all times, is outside holding court with about a dozen campers and spinning old tales.

Before I left, a fellow camper shared my favorite anecdote of the day: An elderly couple from Pittsburgh, en route to Tampa, decided to come to Bradenton to watch Pirates spring training action. They arrived at Pirate City, unaware it's fantasy camp week. After watching us for a few minutes, the wife turned to her husband and said, "I sure hope they get better by April."

Wednesday

After two straight days of baseball and using muscles I haven't thought about in over thirty years, plus some that frankly I didn't know I still had, we all were thrilled to play only one game.

The training room becomes a popular place. Whirlpool, ice, and heat treatments, you name it, just take a number and get in line. I was so sore after playing the doubleheader yesterday that I literally had to pick my legs up with my hands to get them on the bed to join the rest of my body.

By day three, we've fallen into a routine. Mornings started with breakfast in the cafeteria, then off to the clubhouse to put on the white or black uniform for the first game of the day and to swap stories about the games the day before. Then it's off to kangaroo court, some stretching and tossing, and some on-field batting practice which was a really nice touch before the morning games.

While the indoor batting cages are open all day, there is something refreshing and major-league about taking BP on the field before the game. Both teams get about twenty minutes in the cage with the opposition shagging. When we wrap it up, the great Pirate City grounds crew comes on the field, dismantles the batting cage, and then begins to line and prep the field like you would see in any major league stadium on any given game day. It makes all of us feel even more big-league.

Our game today was in downtown Bradenton at McKechnie Field where the Pirates play their spring training games. McKechnie was built in 1923, and the Pirates have been playing there since 1969. It is the oldest spring training stadium in baseball. All teams play one league game at McKechnie, and then we go back on Saturday to play the "Legends" game against the former major leaguers. The stadium holds 6,600 people, was recently renovated, and everyone from Babe Ruth to Ted Williams to Mickey Mantle to Roberto Clemente and, as of this morning, Roy Berger, have played there. On a regular basis it's used by the Bradenton Marauders, the Pirates Class A farm team.

The place is beautiful. We're all kids again for a couple of hours playing ball in a real major-league-caliber stadium. I had to pinch myself. I'm not sure I ever envisioned this moment. Sure, it was a minor league ballpark. And I am no stranger to minor league stadiums, having lived and worked in Tucson, Wichita, and Birmingham, but it was big-league and big-time for the Pirates for six weeks every year, and I was playing in it. It's also the first time I'd ever reported to a minor league stadium in full uniform. All the other times it was with family in tow for a day or night of entertainment. Now, I was the entertainment. Dugouts, umpires, grounds crew, balls, and bats—is this really happening? Don't wake me if it's not. We came into this morning's game at 2–0 and the only undefeated team in our division. The Traynors were 1–1. We left McKechnie a couple of hours later as one of only two 3–0 teams remaining. Despite jumping ahead early at 6–0, we had to hang on for an 8–6 win. It was actually a good game and probably our most competitive. I had a decent day with a hit and a walk in three at-bats, and I didn't hurt the club in the field.

Just before today's game, Virdon looked at me with a grin, and probably sensing my youthful excitement said, "Roy, do you want me to put you in the lineup today?" In my wildest dreams, I'd never expected a Yankees manager (former or not) to ask me that question.

Our starting pitcher again was young Briles. His dad pitched for many years during the spring at McKechnie, and it was a thrill for David to walk out onto the same mound.

The Traynors started a lefty, sixty-year-old Frank Mincarelli. In fact, he's the third lefty I've faced in three days. Normally, a left-handed pitcher to a left-handed hitter match-up favors the pitcher. It's especially true at fifty-seven years old, when the reflexes slow down and you see the ball about a half second too late as it comes to you from a completely different direction. Good thing for me, a sixty-year-old (and not one half his age) was hurling.

I was lucky my first time up against the southpaw and stuck an 0–2 pitch through the left side of the infield for a hit. Second time against Mincarelli I figured I'd wait for something I could clearly see and wound up with a walk, which ultimately led to two runs and the difference in the game.

My third time up was against a fifty-five-year-old righty, Paul Metlin, who only twelve weeks earlier had had quadruple bypass surgery. It was so important for him to be here this week that he accelerated rehab so he could play. I hit a solid line drive that the shortstop had to leap to snag. He also doubled our runner off second. It was one of those shots that should have been a base hit; the one in the first inning, probably not. In baseball, it all evens out.

For our last at-bat in the seventh inning, the Traynors put the oldest camper on the mound to pitch. Wouldn't you know Don Jacobs, seventy-seven years old and here for the eleventh straight year, set us down in order at about forty mph with pinpoint control. Good for him.

There was also a nice turnout in the stands today at McKechnie. When the game started, there was one person in attendance. By the time the game ended, the crowd had at least tripled.

Through three league games, we were 3–0 and I'd gone 4–8 with two walks and four RBIs. It's also no accident I hadn't scored an official run yet. Those bases are really far away from each other, and them legs ain't what they used to be.

Tomorrow we have a doubleheader, which wraps up league play with the top two teams in each division headed to the playoffs. We have already clinched a playoff spot and need one more win to clinch our division. Of course, making the playoffs ultimately means one or two more games and countless swallows of Advil.

Kangaroo court, prior to the trip to McKechnie, featured fines and transgressions from Tuesday. First was the camper who was fined for asking ex-major leaguer Jerry Reuss, "So is this your first fantasy camp as a camper?" The other was assessed to me. Blass said, "Where's Berger?" Uh oh! I had a feeling it was coming. He asked, "How come you didn't wear your Yankees warm-up again this morning?" I guess I wasn't quick enough to get that "NY" covered by my glove yesterday. The Pirates were kind enough to leave a Pirate-logoed warm-up for me in my locker on Tuesday afternoon, so I thought I had better get with the program, and I wore it this morning, but too late to make anyone forget about the Yankees warm-up yesterday.

Blass said my fine was only $1, but I could appeal it. He said he was also the judge for appeals, and if I lost my appeal the fine would be tripled. I shut up, paid the buck, and felt I was $2 and a nice Pirates sweater ahead of the game.

Having the afternoon off was a welcome relief to most. I know I enjoyed it, and I needed my legs to make it all the way downstairs for the evening activity.

On the camp itinerary, it was called the "All-American Cookout," although it was held indoors at the very versatile Pirate City cafeteria, and there was no sign of a barbeque pit. Nonetheless, the food was good and plentiful and was preceded by an interesting hour when, for the first time, there was an organized autograph event.

Campers were encouraged to bring a couple of items to be signed by the ex-big leaguers. We were asked to use discretion and limit the number of items to three. Almost no one followed instructions. You should have seen the stuff guys brought to be signed: balls, bats, baseball cards, yearbooks, ticket stubs, photos, seat cushions, actual framed pictures and plaques, and newspaper stories. One guy brought a chair from the old Forbes Field that he somehow justified schlepping to camp. And then there was the guy walking around with a Forbes Field home plate.

Earlier in the day, the Pirates had left in each of our lockers a nice black baseball bat—a regulation Louisville Slugger, monogrammed with our name and Pittsburgh Pirates 2010 Fantasy Camp, along with a silver Sharpie to be used if we desired an autograph during the evening. It's the only thing I brought with me tonight. As exciting as it was to have my idols sign my bat, my evening was made complete following the autograph session when I saw Mazeroski step outside to smoke his pre-dinner cigar.

In the mid-sixties when we were kids, I used to engage in adolescent sibling rivalry with my brother Mike, who is three years younger than I am. Of course, it revolved around baseball. Mike was a huge Yankees fan despite our dad and me following the Pirates. Each team had its own superstar: Mickey Mantle for the Yanks and the emerging Roberto Clemente for the Bucs, but we never engaged in "who's better" when it came to the studs.

Instead, our very volatile rivalry was at second base. The Yankees had Bobby Richardson who was Mike's hero. My man was Bill Mazeroski. Their stats were incredibly similar. While Richardson was a career .266 hitter in twelve major league seasons and Maz had a .260 lifetime average over seventeen years, it was on defense where they both shined.

Richardson won five Gold Gloves and Maz won eight. Both were chosen to the all-star teams during the height of the Berger brothers' battles circa 1964–67. Both players were at the top of their respective games, and it made our internal feud that much better.

So tonight, I couldn't let the opportunity pass. I followed Maz outside and told him about the knock-down-and-drag-outs Mike and I used to have over who was better—Maz or Richardson?

Maz knew who I was and seemed amused. He said, "Get your brother on the phone for me." When Mike answered, all I said to him was, "I have someone who wants to talk to you," and I handed the phone to the greatest second baseman of all-time.

Maz started the conversation simply: "So you think Bobby Richardson was better than me?" I'm not sure what happened after that as I only heard one side of the debate. My brother is a heck of a salesman, but I doubted even he could pull this one off. About three or four minutes passed and Maz handed me the phone and said, "I just got him straightened out." I took the phone back. Mike said to me, "Well, there is no doubt in his mind that Bobby Richardson was better." It was one of those moments you never can imagine and one you can never get back. Pure fantasy camp erotica.

Ironically, even though Mazeroski was the 1960 World Series hero, Richardson was actually voted Series MVP for his .367 batting average with twelve RBIs. It was the first, and in baseball's long history, still the only time a member of the losing team was chosen Series MVP. Fortunately, Mike was only five years old at the time and has no recollection. As I told my brother over and over, Bill Mazeroski is in the Baseball Hall of Fame, and Bobby Richardson has to buy a ticket to get in. Case closed.

Thursday

Today was another doubleheader day. The Wednesday afternoon of rest was appreciated by all, but it was time to get back to fantasy business again as the last two games of league play remained to decide playoff positions.

The eight teams were divided into two divisions with the top four teams advancing to Friday's playoff/championship game rounds. The top team in Division A meets the second team in Division B and vice versa.

We found out before we played our first game that, to our surprise, we had already won our division. We were 3–0 and everyone else in our bracket was 1–2, so there was no way we could be beaten for the top spot. When Virdon was advised we'd already clinched, he called his first team meeting of the week.

Bill's instructions to us were to play the first game as we normally would and go after it to win. He said we would back off in the afternoon and would let anyone who wanted to try pitching or playing a different position on the field have the opportunity.

Our morning game was against the Cuylers managed by Vernon Law and assisted by Sid Bream. They were 1–2 and already eliminated from the playoffs.

Law, nicknamed "The Deacon" during his playing days for his Mormon heritage, was a twenty-game winner for the Pirates during the 1960 championship season. He also won the Cy Young Award as the best pitcher in the National League in 1960 and was Pirates manager Danny Murtaugh's go-to guy in Game 7 of the World Series. Still a very dignified looking gentleman.

We beat them 18–0 on a windswept day to move to 4–0 and followed manager Virdon's orders. We played hard and chalked up another of those rare camp whitewashes.

I had a very good batting practice before the game, stinging the ball as well as I had since the batting cages at home three months ago. I walked away knowing how the big guys feel when they say they can sense they are going to have a good day. Then came my first at-bat.

Today's game was listed as a "TV" game. The game is recorded with on-the-field commentary and interviews and will be used as part of the commemorative DVD of the week's experience sent to all present and potential campers.

My first at-bat, with cameras rolling, was as bad an at-bat as I've had this week and in the last forty-two years. Figures, doesn't it? Deservedly, I wound up getting called out on strikes, and I felt lost at the plate. Of course, we have film of it. I was none too jolly.

Fortunately, things turned around in a hurry. I walked my second time up; hit a wind-aided blooper single to right with runners on second and third my third time up for an RBI; had a solid single to center my fourth time up; and another single to right-center my fifth time at the plate for another RBI. I also scored two runs. Finally.

I finished the game 3–4 with a walk, two RBIs, two runs scored, and a respectable day in the field. I was selected as one of our three stars of the game and afterwards was held over for an interview for the DVD. Neat stuff.

The wind played tricks all day on the outfielders, and after a while you had to feel bad for the Cuylers as they just couldn't do anything right. Finally, as we went ahead 18–0 in the top of the seventh and had the bases loaded and nobody out, Sid Bream said to heck with the rules, and he came in to pitch for his side.

Bream, fifty, had an eleven-year major league career with the Dodgers, Pirates, Braves, and Astros and was a .264 left-handed hitter with 90 home runs and 455 RBIs. He played in two World Series with the Braves but ironically is perhaps best remembered for scoring the winning run in the 1992 playoff series against none other than the Pirates. He looks like he can still play at an imposing 6'4", 215 pounds, but underneath it all is a real nice guy.

Bream quickly showed us why this week was nothing but a fantasy for us. Even though he was a first baseman by trade, he could pitch better than any of us. With the bases loaded and nobody out, it took him five pitches to retire the side. A combination of smoke and one curve ball that started in Orlando and crossed the plate in Bradenton resulted in a quick double play and vicious strike out. It was fun to watch as long as I didn't have to bat against him, and thankfully, I didn't.

We got what skipper Virdon asked for, and that was a win in what turned out to be a very long game. The only negative was we lost our catcher, Frank Monaco, a sixty-year-old police chief from a community outside of Pittsburgh. He slipped coming out of the batter's box and banged up his knee. He'll be on crutches, which now leaves us with nine players and no room left for any more injuries.

After a quick lunch, we returned to the field. We played the Stargells, managed by Blass and assisted by Mazeroski. Before the game, we found out the Stargells will be our opening playoff opponent on Friday as they clinched second in their division with a 2–2 win-loss record. Virdon told us before the game, "We are going to take this easy and not show 'em too much.'"

We didn't. We let two guys pitch that hadn't thrown before and for the first time all week, we trailed in a game. Falling behind 3–0, we rallied for five runs to take a lead at 5–3 into the bottom of the fourth. We got the first two guys out and then three straight errors led to three runs and a 6–5 lead for the Stargells.

At that point, both teams decided to rest their pitchers and a minor league assistant came in to pitch for each team. The pitch speed was turned up, the intensity turned down, and the game finished in a 6–5 loss for the good guys. Our league record stood at 4–1, at the top of the division going into Friday's playoff round.

I was 0–2 and a walk, but I didn't feel as good as I had earlier in the day. I had popped something in my arm during one of the at-bats and been fighting off a hamstring and quad pull. I finished league play with eight hits, far ahead of what I imagined I would be able to do when I arrived on Sunday. When I got here, one solid base hit would have made my week. I got seven more as a bonus.

The most popular spot this week off the field is the nightly gathering in the makeshift lounge set up for cocktails, poker, old baseball stories, and a cigar or three. Most of the ex-ballplayers stop by each night and some stay much longer than others. I headed up there each night to enjoy my cigar and listen to the stories of the day. There's always a poker game and others huddled around the television watching either college basketball, or more times than not, the MLB Network. Campers and pro staff come and go each night. Considering the ex-major leaguers don't stay at Pirate City but instead at a nearby Marriott, it's a nice touch that they drop by for a visit and a drink.

The second most popular spot is the training room. All week long there has been a steady procession of guys getting rubs, treatments, whirlpool, sauna, and you-name-it for us old hacks. This might be the 1960 Pirates fiftieth anniversary celebration week, but unfortunately none of us are 1960 age anymore and we are feeling it.

My day ended in the training room, too. My arm hurt, I was gimpy on the hamstring/quad, and I sat on a training table for fifteen minutes with an ice wrap around my left arm and another one on my right thigh. For the first time all week, I felt my age plus an additional ten years. My six-day-a-week, four forty-five a.m. cardio exercises at home ignore baseball muscles that haven't been activated in forty years; right now they are very grumpy. Adrenaline and excitement may have gotten me through the first few days, but now with one or maybe two games tomorrow and only nine guys left standing, I've gotta make it through, even if it's only thanks to grit, determination, and gobs of IcyHot.

Friday

Today is playoff day at fantasy camp with the hope that by day's end, all the pulled muscles and bruises and ice treatments and bandages are worth it when the championship trophy is presented.

It was amusing at breakfast to see guys with bad limps, arms in slings, and one on crutches doing their best to struggle to get their waffles from the cafeteria line over to their tables. As one of the guys at our table who is an auditor said, "I don't know if I can play or not today. The only thing that doesn't hurt me is my head." I doubt the same can be said for the fellas who closed the lounge last night.

I actually feel good this morning. Or as good as I could after putting my fifty-seven-year-old body through what I have the past five days. The ice treatments in the training room yesterday really made my hamstring, quads, and arm feel better.

Kangaroo court is uneventful with the exception of the gutsy gent who went over to say hello to His Honor, Blass, and gave him a pat on the back. Along with that pat was some masking tape that covered the B and L on the back of Blass's uniform. So

Steve Blass became Steve Ass this morning and he had absolutely no idea. Every time he turned around, it was there for all to see. It went on for a good fifteen minutes as he couldn't figure out why everyone was snickering. Finally, someone convinced him to take off his shirt and take a look. It was priceless. The culprit has not been apprehended. What goes around comes around.

All teams are in action this morning with only the top four qualifying for the playoff round. The other four teams played a round robin, for those who felt up to it.

Final stats were posted for regular league play, and I was very surprised at my line—eight hits in fourteen at-bats, seven RBIs, three walks, and two runs scored. The .571 average is second best on the team. My performance far exceeds anything I could have imagined a week ago, and our manager Bill Virdon batted me fifth in this morning's lineup, a spot I really couldn't have envisioned being placed, as the last time I played or hit a hardball was forty-two years ago in 1968.

Our catcher, Monaco, was on crutches at breakfast, but ninety minutes later, the crutches were gone and he took batting practice. Thirty minutes into the game, he laced a single to left field as our DH. Hey, it's the fantasy camp playoffs and it's all-in.

Fortunately, the wind is blowing from left to right this morning as Maz coached first base with a huge lit cigar and the fumes blew away from, rather than right at me. If the wind switched direction at any point during the game, I would have become the only first baseman in baseball history to develop a mild case of emphysema while on the field. Still, it was a lot of fun to have Maz coaching for seven innings at first base, and I had a chance to gab with one of my childhood heroes.

I was feeling okay until my first at-bat when the stride tweaked the hamstring again and my upper arm got knotted when I made contact with the ball. Then, our infielders' arms started playing tricks on them, so I had a very interesting and challenging game fielding throws at first while trying to stretch a leg that didn't want to be stretched.

The game itself was a good one; in fact, the best of the week. It had a completely different feel than any other game as it was very tense. The Stargells took a 1–0 lead into the bottom of the fourth when we scored a run to tie it. It stayed 1–1 until the bottom of the seventh when we loaded the bases with one out. Briles then popped out to third.

Bases loaded, two outs, tie game, last inning. We need a doctor. No, nothing's wrong, but a forty-year-old family practice physician from Butler, Pennsylvania, was the answer. Dr. Mike Fiorina promptly laced a single to center to give us a 2–1 win, clearing our bench in celebration as en masse we all limped out to mob Dr. Fiorina and then hobbled to the training room for treatment before the afternoon championship game.

At lunch, I ask Virdon to drop me down some in the order for the finale. I'm having a problem striding, and I don't want to hurt the team. He told me he moved me to the bottom. I said, "Skip, I said drop me, not plunge me." He laughed, saw the error of his ways, and moved me back up a few spots for the title game.

Before the game, with the line in the training room looking like a half-price sale at Wal-Mart, I go back up to my room to apply some IcyHot to ease the aches. I find out very quickly if you are going to use IcyHot for the hamstrings, you must be very, very careful where you apply it. Stay away from the inner thigh.

We play the Clementes in the championship game. They are clearly the class team of camp. They come into the final with a 6–0 record, including a 10–1 win in the morning playoff game, and didn't even use their two best pitchers. We were 5–1 and had to use everything we had to beat the Stargells.

The Clementes are coached by former Pirates infielder Dave Cash and 1960 World Series pitcher Joe Gibbon, who was also a basketball All-American at Ole Miss in 1957.

Joe Klimchak is the host of the pre-game entertainment for the Pirates at PNC Park in Pittsburgh for all Pirates home games. He has been at fantasy camp this week doing interviews with campers and commentary on game action for the DVD we'll all receive in a couple of months. I asked Joe for the betting line on the championship game. He favored the Clementes by five runs. Personally, I thought that might be a bit light as they'd had no trouble with anyone all week. And unlike Pete Rose, who claims to never have bet against his own team, I have to tell you laying the five run spread was pretty tempting.

It was fun to look in the stands and see Vern Law and Bob Friend sitting together watching the game. They combined for thirty-eight wins as the stalwarts of the 1960 World Championship pitching staff, and there was no situation ever in my mind that would have put them watching me play a baseball game. Most of the campers came out for a while to take a look before heading to the golf course, beach, or to catch a nap, and the other pros also made a respectful appearance.

We jumped out to an early 1–0 lead behind our ace Kevin Kubala and that was it for us. The Clementes put together four runs in the middle three innings for a 4–1 win and the title.

Though we were on the wrong side, we did get to see the best pitcher in camp, forty-four-year-old David Gibbon, who happens to be Joe's son and had pitched some college ball back in his day.

The Clementes brought Gibbon in to pitch the last three innings to protect their lead. Nine up and nine down. Velocity somewhere around eighty mph and not many out of the strike zone. I think I saw three pitches from him breeze by me. Quite a contrast from the fifty to fifty-five mph we had been facing most of the week.

If we hadn't been on the receiving end, it would have been fun to watch. They were better and deserved to win. As a reward, they get to play first on Saturday when we go back to McKechnie Field for our three-inning game against the Pirate Legends. Our team will play second, and each of the eight teams in camp will get to play three innings against the former big leaguers.

As we head back to the clubhouse, dejected but not totally surprised, I want to make sure I catch up to Bill Virdon to thank him for his patience with this camp rookie. It was an honor to play for him not only because of his baseball accomplishments and the role he played in my youth, but also because he is an absolute gentleman. Mr. Virdon looked me right in the eye through his trademark glasses and said without hesitation, "Roy, I guarantee you I had more fun this week than you did." I highly doubt that, sir.

I will leave fantasy camp play with a very respectable batting average, and the championship game was probably my most challenging defensively, filled with constant activity. With no flexibility in either my arm or my hamstrings, and little reflexes left, I didn't hurt my team in the field. And maybe the best news of the day is that we covered the spread in the title game. After all, that's what it's really all about.

Tonight, after our runner-up finish, was our team dinner. We took our coaching staff out as a thank-you for their patience all week. Pete Hoffman, at his tenth straight camp, picked the restaurant. The place came highly recommended by both Sid Bream and Mike LaValliere, so we trusted it would be good.

As a side note, it's ironic these two were in camp together this week. One of the most infamous plays in Pirates history was their loss in the 1992 NLCS playoff series to Atlanta when Bream, a Brave at the time, slid around LaValliere's tag to score the winning run in the seventh game of the series to beat Pittsburgh and advance to the World Series. Pirates fans haven't gotten over it nor pardoned ex-Pirate Bream, who still lives in Pittsburgh, and despite six years as a Pirate in the late eighties, he has anti-hero status in his hometown. The Pirates have been on a consecutive season losing streak ever since the "Curse of Bream."

Virdon said he would meet us at the restaurant as did Pete Birbilis, a camper who resides in the Bradenton area. The rest of us, including coach Jerry Reuss, left from the dorm at Pirate City.

Once we finally found the place, we knew we had been punked by Bream and LaValliere. The Havana Cabana was more of a coffee house than a restaurant. A piano player of marginal skill tortured the ivories in the corner and I could only see six other people eating.

The menu was sandwiches and burgers, but thankfully, the Havana Cabana also served alcohol. A couple of our guys had spent the afternoon consuming beverages after our championship game loss, and they were able to keep everyone's spirits up.

Virdon, his wife Shirley, and Birbilis were no-shows, which was disappointing even if this restaurant wasn't the "thank-you" we had in mind. We ate, it was terrible, and by the time the bill came, we all felt we were in Fenway Park as we did a "Sweet Caroline" sing-along, more out of self-pity than enjoyment.

I ran into Virdon at breakfast the next morning and told him he had made a wise choice not showing up last night.

He looked at me quizzically and said, "Are you kidding? I was at the right place and dinner was excellent." It turns out that our van driver confused the Havana Cabana with the Banana Cabana, where we missed a great dinner enjoyed by Virdon, Shirley, and the local guy who knew a banana from a havana.

Saturday

Before the Saturday Legends games kicked off, the official stats for the week were released and we discovered we were no-hit in the championship game the day before. We lost 4–1, never realized we didn't have a hit, but our only run scored on a walk, error, and sac fly.

For the week, while we finished 5–2 and made the title game, we were the second-worst hitting team of the eight in camp. We batted .340 which only topped the .281 by a team that only won one game. The Clementes, undefeated at 7–0, batted .514.

If our offense was among the worst at camp, our defense was among some of the best. We had at least one double play in each game and were very strong up the middle as most putouts in camp come at second base. We were very good in the infield. If you can't hit you probably need to stop the other guys and we did that well; in fact, the best of any team in camp, as evidenced by our two rare shutout wins.

Looking at the final stats, my week was very good despite being a not-so-clutch 0–5 in the playoffs. I was credited with eight hits in nineteen at-bats for a .421 average and seven RBIs. It was the second highest average on the team next to Kubala, who hit .583. I really didn't envision stats like this a week ago.

My goal was to survive the week without undue humiliation and by and large, I succeeded. I got a few hits, played okay in the field, and now after forty-two years, I can put the glove back into storage when I get home.

We returned downtown to McKechnie Field Saturday morning to play against the Legends. As we arrived at the park, it was impressive to see a long line of people outside the stadium seemingly ready for the gates to open. We were a bit humbled. That feeling didn't last very long as we found out that tickets for the Pirates pre-season games went on sale in an hour and both the Yankees and Red Sox were coming to Bradenton in a month, but darn, it felt big-time for about five minutes.

We played a simulated major league game against the Legends. An announcer made introductions over the PA system and even a few hundred spectators filtered into the stadium. Some were friends and family of the campers who came to take pictures while there was a large contingent of locals seeking to get autographs from the ex-Pirates. Each of the eight teams play three innings with everyone getting at least one at-bat against former major league pitching. The Legends' inning would end when either the side was retired or they scored three runs.

As my team finished second overall, we were penciled in to play the pros in the second game. It was pretty special to be standing at first base and realize Rennie Stennett was at the plate, though it did get a bit scary when lefty LaValliere was at bat, and downright intimidating when southpaw Bream, still as imposing as ever, came up. I was just hoping I wouldn't get hurt.

I found myself daydreaming as I smoothed the dirt with my foot at first base. Here I am wearing a major league uniform, staring down at ex-major league ballplayers. I came back to my senses pretty quickly with the row of left-handed batters at the plate, but a big part of me wanted my dad sitting in the stands, watching. I knew pictures and a phone call would have to suffice. The ballpark was alive with people and music and baseball. For a fleeting second I could make believe.

At-bat we faced forty-nine-year-old Zane Smith, who pitched all three innings for the Legends. Zane had 100 career wins in a twelve-year span pitching for Pittsburgh, Atlanta, Montreal, and Boston.

He threw fastballs down the middle. Even though he'd retired fourteen years ago, he still threw about seventy to eighty mph; all I wanted to do was make contact. His speed was tough enough, and it didn't help me trying to pick the ball up off a lefthander.

I saw a ball and a strike on the first two pitches and slapped the ball to third on the next pitch. In another bang-bang play at first, I was out by a close ten steps. I succeeded. I hit the ball off the first major league pitcher I ever faced.

We went ten up and ten down. None of the eight teams scored a run off the Legends all day. They scored nine runs in the three innings against us, and I took off my uniform knowing I had accomplished everything, and probably a little more than, I had hoped during the week. Frankly, I couldn't wait to return home to my wife, my dog, and my regular life. Even though this had been a great experience and the completion of a childhood dream, I looked forward to never opening another tube of IcyHot. Putting on a suit and tie Monday morning sounds like a welcome reprieve.

The closing banquet was a great way to finish. Each team was called up to the podium. Coaches offered their parting words, thoughts, and took some last shots at us. We were each given a signed baseball and really nice 1960 World Championship commemorative plaque. Campers who had returned to camp every year for the past five or ten years were also honored with a special video tribute.

Most special of all was the acknowledgment given to the solo ball-playing female of the week, a very nice and attractive woman named Julie Seidman of Manhattan Beach, California. Julie, forty-eight, had just completed her tenth straight Pirates camp with her dad, Don Jacobs, who had been inducted into the ten-year class a year earlier.

Julie came to Bradenton for the first time eleven years ago to watch Don play. As Julie recalled, "My dad signed up, and I flew down to watch him and make sure he didn't get hurt. After watching, it seemed like so much fun that I sent in a deposit the next year, and I've been coming back ever since."

She first attended camp in 2000 and had to choose a position, although she had never really played baseball or softball. "After watching for a while," Julie said, "I decided I wanted to be a catcher, because it appeared all you had to do is stick your glove out and the ball would come right into it." I'm not sure Johnny Bench or Thurman Munson shared that simplistic sentiment, but it seems to have worked for Ms. Seidman, who learned to play ball and batted .238 for camp with five hits in twenty-one at-bats. Her dad found the going a little tougher at seventy-seven with one hit in fifteen at-bats and more credit than you can garner in a big bushel for suiting up this week.

In a way, I identified with Julie. I came to camp to follow a lifelong dream that started fifty years ago and was locked away in a storage closet most likely never to see the light of day. Julie came to watch her father; I came because of my father. I was there to honor my bond with my father and what he instilled in me as not only a baseball fan, but also as the son of a baseball fan. I tried to pass along that honor and respect for the game through the years with my two boys as well; now Jason and Scott are big baseball guys, too. It was really nice to tie a bow around three generations in one week of camp. As a bonus, I got to play and socialize with heroes of my past in a scenario I could have never dreamed would happen.

The evening ended with a moving video tribute to the 1960 World Championship team, the honorees for the week. Mazeroski closed the camp by wiping a tear from his eye and saying, "Somebody probably brings up the home run to me six days a week. I can't believe it's held up for fifty years. I get far too much credit than I deserve...we won as a team." Then there was a thunderous standing ovation for the entire 1960 team—by those of us who could actually still stand.

I knew I was a Pirates fan because of my dad. He became a Pirates fan because he liked the Waner brothers—Paul Waner, known as "Big Poison," and his brother Lloyd, known as "Little Poison." Dad said, "They were Pirates, so I became a Pirates fan."

My room in Pirate City this week, room 205, was the Paul Waner room.

Some weeks are meant to be.

The headquarters and dorm building at Pirate City.

My first big-league uniform and locker.

An honor to play for Bill Virdon.

Making contact at McKechnie Field.

Facing my first major league pitcher—Zane Smith.

The 1960 World Champions (l–r): Bill Mazeroski, Vern Law, Joe Gibbon, Bob Skinner, Bill Virdon, Bob Oldis, and Bob Friend.

Fourth Inning

Start Slow and Taper Off

January 2011

*T*he week at Pirates camp was fantastic. It was all that was promised and more. Over half of the eighty-three campers were repeat attendees, which I didn't understand at first. Someone told me, "It's like a drug, you'll see." I got hooked in about three days and couldn't wait to lace 'em up again.

The state of contentment to return to the suit and tie and real life after Pirates camp lasted about two weeks. Once I stopped having to use chairs, tables, and walls to hold onto while I walked, the thought of reliving the week I had just finished returned. As we get older, our fantasies change, and in your late fifties, you are no longer dreaming about something unobtainable or unapproachable. At least not me. My daydreams were about another week playing baseball.

I discovered the date of next year's Pirates camp conflicted with my company's annual meeting, so I'd miss the after-dinner cigar with Bill Mazeroski and realized if I wanted to do it again, I would have to branch out.

Of course, as a die-hard Yankees fan, my first thought was to revisit the idea of New York Yankees camp. The Yankees camp would be a very special experience that I would ideally share with my brother Mike, who while younger, has been a Yankees fan longer than I have.

But Mike had multiple conflicts, not the least of which was paying college tuition for his twins. That conversation turned into a short one. I had the bug and wanted to play ball somewhere and still was a little intimidated at the prospect of going it alone in Yankeeland. That experience has much more appeal with a companion joining me and appreciating how special it is. So, I did a little research and stumbled upon Detroit Tigers camp in Lakeland, Florida—the longtime spring home of the real Tigers.

From the website, it appeared the Tigers have this fantasy camp stuff down to a science. It is the oldest of all the camps. The upcoming camp would be the twenty-eighth year, and it's so popular that they run back-to-back weeks to satisfy the demand. In fact, almost two hundred campers over the next fortnight would pony up big bucks to be a Tiger for a week.

Camp director Jerry Lewis couldn't have been nicer or more accommodating. I had the Tigers brochure within a week, and Jerry wanted to learn as much about my Pirates experience as he could. The $3,400 price seemed like a value.

I just wanted to play ball and the date and moving parts seemed to be a fit. I have no affiliation or sentiment at all with the Detroit Tigers. Never cared for them much, but more importantly, they don't raise the ire in my sights as Boston does. I also figured if former Yankee Johnny Damon could don a Tiger uniform last year, I could this year.

Now that I had found my spot, I really wanted a sidekick to join me. The Pirates week solo was fine, and while I certainly made some on-the-field friendships, many times I really did feel like a lonesome rookie. I got lucky. After hearing of my exploits last year, Peter Evans, a just-turned fifty-year-old travel insurance executive and colleague from Madison, Connecticut, offered to join me. It wasn't idle chatter; we sent in our deposits at the same time.

So we made our plans to head to Tigertown in Lakeland, a quick forty-five minutes from Orlando. It will be nice to share the experience with a guy who could laugh at an error and not be real concerned with the final score.

There's only one thing about Pete that troubles me.

I prepared for this camp as I did a year ago, before my rookie experience. I did some throwing while vacationing in Florida with my sons, I visited a local indoor batting cage regularly on weekends, and I spent some time with the University of Alabama at Birmingham (UAB) baseball training staff on stretching exercises to keep the legs moving. I remember how badly that hamstring ached after the final game last year, and how far apart those bases seemed to be from each other. I asked Pete if he'd been preparing. "Yep," he said. "Went out and bought a new pair of socks, watched an old baseball game on ESPN Classic, and been chewing some bubble gum."

Should be an interesting week.

Sunday

Day one, Sunday afternoon, is orientation day for all the aging Tigers. Enrollment hit ninety-one campers, representing twelve states, and included five women. The average age for this session is fifty-two, which puts me again on the upper tier.

Of the ninety-one campers, an incredible 60 percent are returnees. We have some that have been here for sixteen, seventeen, eighteen, and twenty consecutive years. The dean of all fantasy campers, Jerry Kruso, is at his thirty-first annual week, including some back-to-backers. He could be the originator of the fantasy camp mantra: "It's like a drug, you'll see." Clearly, Jerry just can't get enough.

Jim Price, a former Tigers catcher and now broadcaster and camp co-director, told us the message for the week was "start slow and taper off." He wasn't kidding.

The parade of former big leaguers who serve as our mentors were introduced; they all have pretty stellar Tiger backgrounds. On hand were Dave Bergman, Darrell Evans, John Grubb, Dan Petry, Dave Rozema, Jon Warden (who doubles as kangaroo court judge), Frank Tanana, Larry Herndon, Tony Phillips, Jack Billingham, and the big Tiger bopper Willie Horton. Detroit legend and Hall of Famer Al Kaline was camp honoree, though he's only scheduled to be on hand for a day.

Teams are revealed during the opening banquet, obviously chosen by the staff in advance. Pete and I would play together on a team managed by former major league star Darrell Evans, who hit 414 home runs in twenty big league seasons, and Frank Tanana, a once hard-throwing lefthander with 240 career wins.

Things start with clinics and pictures in the morning and opening games in the afternoon. I remembered three things I learned last year at Pirates camp to be kept foremost in mind:

1. If IcyHot is used on the hamstrings and quads, it's probably a real good idea if you don't rub your inner thighs together while walking. I was hoppin' around at first base like the proverbial Mexican jumping bean of days long gone and feeling like an ant colony was inside my pants. No inner leg application. Please.

2. Take a duffel bag to carry your glove and other accessories you might need on the field. I didn't know this little tidbit last season, and while the Pittsburgh guys were all marching to the field with totes, duffel bags, and even some larger bags to carry their bats, I was an aging, balding first baseman with a Westin Hotel laundry bag. I might as well have had a sign pinned on my back that said "camp rook." It was a bit embarrassing. On day two or three, I even went to a local Dollar Store to look for a duffel bag, but all they had were these wonderful prints and styles of palm trees ready for a day on the beach. I couldn't do it and rode the week out with my plastic laundry bag. So for this year's camp, I had to make a decision: take a duffel bag or upgrade to a trendy Peninsula Hotel canvas laundry bag. I brought the duffel and told Pete, "If you do nothing else this week, bring a duffel bag."

3. Remember that the older you get, the further apart the bases seem. That was a long run to first base last year and now that I was a year older, I was thinking it would probably seem three or four steps farther this year. I

decided to subscribe to the Southwest Airlines philosophy for running the bases: point to point. Go from first to second. Stop and refuel. Go from second to third. Stop, grab a drink, and refuel. Final destination is home plate. You can eventually get there, but don't pass up a chance to rest en route. Southwest will never pass one airport without stopping and refueling. Same for me running the bases. If for any reason I need to go non-stop from first to third, I'd be calling a cab.

Last year with the Pirates, my goal for the week was to not feel embarrassed doing something I hadn't done in forty-seven years. My hope was to get one base hit in a real game and be satisfied. That hit came early in our first game.

This year my goal is simple: have a good time and relish the opportunity. As a kid, you want to play in the major leagues but very, very few get that chance. So my goal is to enjoy being with Pete and not to take a moment for granted. My expectation is to return to the airport on Sunday morning without a medical escort.

Monday

Despite my optimistic outlook, the baseball-playing week got off to a very inauspicious start.

Report time for day one of the schedule was to be in the Tigers clubhouse Monday by nine a.m., make sure our uniforms fit, and be ready for stretching and clinics by nine thirty. Pete and I decided we'd head over early and left the not-so-posh Lakeland Inn and Conference Center an hour early. I remembered the special feeling last year of walking into a major league clubhouse and seeing my uniform with my name and number hanging from my locker for the very first time. Truly an adoring baseball fan's dream.

We made our way to the clubhouse at the Tigertown complex and found we were housed on the same row of lockers. Pete's white home and gray away uniforms hung neatly from their perch with his chosen #8 and last name "Evans" emblazoned on both sets of shirts. Pete stands 5'4" so he is a tailor's nightmare. My #56 was likewise hanging just down the row. I had a good rookie camp with the Pirates, so why tempt fate and change numbers?

When I saw my uniform and locker, I realized that the excitement I had growing up a Pittsburgh Pirates fan and living the same experience a year ago was missing this morning. Not having a Detroit Tigers passion or affinity made the moment rather perfunctory. Kind of been there, done that. I'm here to enjoy playing ball for a week, and the uniform is just part of the tools.

I immediately looked over at Pete's locker to see his reaction. What I hoped might be a little youthful giddiness at his major league unveiling was a bit matter-of-fact. Pete is the type who has never met a stranger, and he was gabbing with those around him like he hadn't seen them in fifty years, which actually was the case. I also learned that Pete is more of an active participant than a passive sports fan. He would rather be on the tennis, squash, or racquetball courts or playing golf than sitting and watching a ball game on TV. His baseball allegiance is pretty vanilla for a guy living in Connecticut rooting for both the Mets and the Yankees; something no true New York baseball fan would ever admit. Pete's goal for the week was to have a good time upon my recommendation of this camp, and he wanted to spend the week with me. Pretty flattering.

One important difference between last year's camp and this one quickly became very apparent: just how nice the clubhouse facility was at Pirate City. The contrast with the Tigers' clubhouse was startling. The Pirates' was new, bright, and attractive. They had an ample supply of baseball basics: bubble gum and sunflower seeds available for the taking. There were drums filled with bottled water, soft drinks, and multiple flavors of Powerade to take to the fields or grab on your way back in.

By contrast, the Tigers' facility is faded and old but at least it has a water fountain. Rather than the gleaming trims, fresh fluffy towels, spacious lockers, and sophisticated medical room, this drab enclosure seems more like a high school locker room than a major league clubhouse.

As it turned out, it wasn't major league at all. The big league Tigers clubhouse is over at Joker Marchant Stadium where they play their spring games. The stadium is adjacent to the complex we were using, which is the minor league facility. So much for the "entire major league experience" for the week.

We were introduced to a gentleman who goes by the name Ghost. Ghost is the Tigers' clubhouse manager. Clearly, Ghost had not kept up with the events of the past thirty years because it seems he had no knowledge the Iron Curtain has come down. He was a one-man dictatorship who ruled with an iron fist. Ghost clearly spelled out the rules and regs expected in "his" clubhouse, and there was no margin for error. If we were guests for the week, you could have fooled most of us. We were treated as inmates. The biggest transgression we could violate was that at no time could we wear baseball shoes in the clubhouse. Every time we went back and forth to the field or the street, off came our shoes. I still don't get it.

We got dressed, made sure everything fit (Pete's did!), were given our matching home and away caps, and went outside to throw; something I hadn't done in about three weeks. For Pete, it'd been about twenty-five years.

We played a few minutes of catch with about thirty other campers before the sky darkened and then opened up with rain. A downpour continued for about six hours and washed away opening day.

Rather than play outside, as we all looked forward to doing, we had clubhouse clinics with the ex-major leaguers on pitching, infield, and outfield basics followed by a nice question-and-answer session that most of the Detroit campers truly enjoyed.

Then the teams took turns in the indoor batting range. When our team, led by Darrell not Pete Evans and Tanana, got into the cage, it was impressive to see. We have some big sluggers—or so it looked from BP. But as I told some of our guys, you don't clinch a playoff spot in batting practice. I learned in Pirates camp that a good defense is just as important—maybe even more so at camp—as a good offense. Before a Pirates game last January, we watched the other team take batting practice with our jaws open in amazement. One batter after another just blistered the ball. There was no mercy. It shook us up just standing and watching.

Then the game started. Seven innings later, we beat them 18–0.

So what you see isn't necessarily what you get. We'd have a much better indication of what kind of team we have tomorrow. The Monday afternoon games were rescheduled to Thursday, originally left open as a rehabilitation afternoon. We now have doubleheaders on Tuesday, Wednesday, and Thursday, weather permitting, with at least two and perhaps three games on playoff Friday. My legs are already threatening to catch an early flight home.

It was nice to watch Pete get into the batting cage for the first time in a couple dozen years. After he figured out he wasn't swinging a nine-iron to 125 yards, he made solid contact with the ball and then became a big shot. He wanted me to take him shopping for batting gloves. He went for twenty-five years without batting gloves, hits two solid line drives, and now he thinks he's Alan Trammell.

Dinner tonight was memorabilia night for the campers with all the ex-Tigers available to sign the myriad of baseball cards, pictures, and more that these guys brought with them. Since neither Pete nor I are particularly fans of the Tigers, we opted to sign our autographs on receipts for a nice dinner in Lakeland.

Despite spending our first meal away from camp, I already noticed how welcoming and gracious these Detroit campers are to us first-timers. Last year in Pirates camp, 60 percent of the campers were returnees, and it tended to feel a bit cliquish. Rookies hung with rookies. Already, I've met two guys here from the same town I grew up in on Long Island, and one of them presently lives less than a half mile from my youngest brother. Whether it was their first time back or the tenth, they were all warm, welcoming, and happy to befriend the rookies.

Autograph night must have run long because after dinner, Pete and I were the first ones back to the hotel lounge. The host hotel, Lakeland Inn and Conference Center, was a Holiday Inn in its previous life, but somewhere along the line, they lost the Holiday Inn flag. Considering what a tired franchise Holiday Inn has become, you can just imagine the product that's left for the Lakeland Inn. A one-night stay would be just about enough for anyone. We were booked for a week.

The hotel lounge quickly became the center of the camp universe. Cocktails and good conversation seemed to make the inclement weather and less-than-stellar accommodations bearable. The lounge leader was former Tigers hurler Dave Rozema. Rosey, now fifty-three, was a solid major leaguer with a career record of 60–53 in ten seasons and an ERA of 3.47. He pitched eight years for Detroit, starting with his rookie season in 1977 and finishing out his last two years with Texas, but left no doubt his heart was with the Tigers, sporting the Detroit "D" prominently tattooed on his right forearm. As much as he may have been known for his off-speed stuff, he had also developed quite the reputation as a flake. Repeated incidents helped solidify that persona.

It was May 1982, in a game against the Minnesota Twins in Tiger Stadium. Detroit batters Enos Cabell and Chet Lemon were brushed back and Lemon was hit by a pitch from Twins pitcher Pete Redfern. Inevitably, a brawl started. Rozema came charging from the Tiger dugout intent on delivering a karate kick to a Minnesota player. Unfortunately, Rozema kicked and missed then fell to the ground writhing in pain with a twisted knee. Once the dust settled, Rozema was carted from the field on a stretcher. His best friend, teammate Kirk Gibson, later won the game on a walk-off extra-innings homer. But the damage was done. The next day, Rozema had surgery on the knee and was out for the remainder of the season.

The infamous karate kick wasn't the only goofy episode of Rosey's career. Once, Gibson shoved Rozema off his stool in the Tiger clubhouse. Rozema had a glass bottle of cough syrup in his back pocket, and after landing on it, had to have stitches in his posterior. Allegedly, there was also the time Rosey overslept and missed the team bus after judging a wet T-shirt contest the night before. How about the time he smashed a bar glass in all-star Trammell's face, which resulted in forty-seven stitches? Rozema remains the "butt" of jokes dating back to some of the airheaded moves he made as a young Tiger farmhand, including the time he washed his new car with Brillo pads.

The lounge activity centered on Rosey, who lives in Detroit and works as an ambassador for the Tigers. He always had a drink in his hand and a quip loud enough to be heard throughout the bar. His character was good-natured and everyone knew what to expect, but one of these days, he's liable to find a female camper or a lady bartender who may not take too kindly to his brand of flirting or off-color language, and the Tigers may be looking at harassment and discrimination troubles. The other Tigers would stroll in, have a drink, tell a story, and shake their heads with a "that's Rosey" kind of look. If he were my employee, I'd recognize his role and reinforce his consumer value but would have him take some of it down a notch, as trouble is at the doorstep.

Pete and I grabbed a couple of seats at the bar and waited for the rest of the camp to return. We were soon joined by Ike Blessitt, the camp batting coach. Blessitt's major league career was brief: five at-bats in four games in 1972 for the Tigers. Blessitt, now sixty-one, was regaling us with stories from his days in the Mexican League. It was apparent from his tales and the confirmation of others he was somewhat of a legend for twenty years in that circuit, but could never break out into a major league career. Suddenly—and out of nowhere—Blessitt's stories went from hitting to pitching to me and Pete the idea of becoming financial backers in a baseball academy he wanted to open in Detroit. It got a little uncomfortable. Fortunately, the bar filled up with other campers and Ike left us to take his prospectus to friendlier pockets. It also was the last time anyone saw Blessitt for the next three days. A stomach bug kept him in bed, which wiped out morning batting practice as well. We had no further investment opportunity conversations with Blessitt.

One thing became very apparent tonight—modern technology has no use for baseball history. Following dinner just a few miles from the hotel, Pete and I set the GPS to get us back to Tigertown, located appropriately enough on Al Kaline Drive. As we approached the complex, the female GPS voice told us to "turn left on Alkaline Drive." I wasn't sure whether to turn left or keep driving to look for a six-pack of Duracells.

Tuesday

We awoke Tuesday morning to the news that a late Monday night thunderstorm had swept through Lakeland. When combined with the rain during the day on Monday, which had wiped out our afternoon games, it was a record for the date with over two inches falling.

As we left the hotel for the Tigers complex about a mile away, it was foggy with a light mist, but the forecast was for sunny skies and temps in the mid-seventies. We arrived at the clubhouse and were instructed to put on our uniforms for the morning games.

Nobody was sure if the fields would be playable. We did some throwing, and by nine a.m., we got word that the morning games would be canceled due to unplayable fields. I had to concur; the outfield was slippery and the infield was too muddy for play. I was not only disappointed that the week had started off so badly, but also embarrassed that I'd dragged Pete along for this rather bumpy ride. We were only two days in and it was pretty apparent this was going to be a lot less fun than Pirates camp.

The Tiger brass tried to overcome the second day of disappointment and promised to do their best to get the fields ready for the afternoon games at two. Because our play was cut short, kangaroo court started early. The judge was Jon Warden, a lefthander who pitched one season in the major leagues in 1968 for Detroit's World Championship team. If you are going to play one year in the bigs, you might as well get a ring for your troubles. He appeared in twenty-eight games with a four win, one loss record, eleven saves, and a 3.62 ERA. Arm trouble followed, he was shipped to the Mets, and was never seen again on the mound.

Dressed in a judicial robe and a long, flowing white wig, he held court in a garden area right outside the clubhouse. There were no on-field indiscretions to fine anyone with because we hadn't played any games. Most of it revolved around uniform shortcomings such as missed belt loops, zippers left open, and the like. All proceeds went to The Tigers Foundation for Children. You could appeal, but if you lost the appeal, which is pretty much guaranteed, the fine tripled. Warden, now sixty-three, was also the appellate judge and proudly told us that nobody has ever won an appeal.

I got popped for $4: $2 for wearing a Yankees pullover on Monday, and then another $2 for showing up with a Pirates sweater this morning. Warden was kind enough to reduce my fine when he learned I chose Tigers camp over the Pirates this winter. Being a gentleman, he reduced my fine to $3.99. Seriously.

To fill the morning void, each team was sent to the indoor batting pavilion for an hour with our coaches. Tanana tossed some soft batting practice, and Evans, sixty-two years old with over 400 home runs in his pocket, gave us swing tips. Darrell had put on a few pounds over the years, but is still just about as recognizable as his baseball cards. He lives in Southern California and runs baseball schools. His hitting tips are something you just can't get anywhere else, especially on a rainy day, and since the fields are unplayable, at least we got in some baseball time and did something more productive than heading back to the paradise inn.

Tanana, fifty-seven, is retired and still lives outside of Detroit. He donates much of his time to the church after a twenty-one-year major league career that produced 240 wins and 2,773 strikeouts. He was a first round draft choice of the California Angels in 1971 and also spent time with Boston, Detroit, Texas, the Mets, and Yankees. He made three all-star appearances, and in 1975 not only recorded seventeen strikeouts in one game, but also led the league in Ks.

Tanana is very comfortable in his own skin, and he holds the dubious distinction of being only one of two pitchers to give up home runs to both Hank Aaron and Barry Bonds (the other was Rick Reuschel). After admitting to that he said, "And I'll tell you something else: no American League pitcher gave up more home runs in a career than I did!" He also is the second fantasy camp coach I've had in as many years who carries a nickname bestowed by Chris Berman of ESPN. Last year it was Jerry "Rolls" Reuss. This year it's Frank Tanana "Daiquiri."

If you've ever heard the expression "restless campers," it defined the clubhouse after lunch. As was forecast, at two o'clock it was seventy-six degrees and the sun was shining. The City of Lakeland owns Tigertown and the Tigers rent the complex. Field maintenance is the responsibility of Lakeland, and they decided they didn't want anyone on the fields during the afternoon to give it one solid baking to limit any potential damage with hopes it would be ready for Wednesday.

The games were canceled, uniforms came off again, and a revamped schedule was posted. There were grumbles everywhere, even from the most upbeat and optimistic of campers. Now all teams would play that night at historic Henley Field, located in downtown Lakeland. It's even older than some of the campers.

The good news was we finally get to play. The not-so-good news for me is that our game was scheduled for nine fifteen p.m., a time of evening I don't see very often. Normally by then I have taken my best friend Ibis out on the front lawn to do his final business of the day, and I'm forty-five minutes from ending mine. I wasn't sure how I would pull this one off. We are the third of three games, which meant starting at nine fifteen would be hopeful at best. All of the games have been reduced to five innings, which would move things along a little quicker.

We finally got underway at about nine thirty, and as the clock struck eleven, we closed it down with a 9–3 win over a team coached by former catcher Jim Price and legend Willie Horton. I got the first hit of the season my first time up on the second pitch I saw through the middle for a single. The pitcher was about fifty pounds overweight and forty of it was in his gut. By the time he reached down to try and field my poke, it was past him; nevertheless, it felt good, and a hit is a hit. My second time up, with the bases loaded, I grounded back to the box and this time he snagged it. I got another chance with the bases loaded in my third at-bat and walked. Opening night line for me was a hit in two official appearances—a walk and an RBI.

Pete's first official time with a bat in his hands in twenty-five years was humorous. He had been warned by me as well as some of his cronies from back home in Connecticut to make sure he stretched regularly, as he will be using muscles he normally doesn't. He pooh-poohed us all and said how fit and how quick he was from playing tennis, paddle tennis, and racquetball.

He grounded to third and sure enough popped a hamstring on the way to first. He went down like he had a blowout, but got back up, and even though he forced me out at third, he was able to gimp to first to avoid the double play. A pinch runner was summoned and a visit to the trainer was ordered.

I wanted to laugh and tell him "I told you so," but I honestly felt for him. The trainer told Pete to ice the hamstring and come for a visit in the morning. He stayed in the game as campers tend to do if they can still walk. In his second at-bat, he put one right through the middle for his maiden camp hit. He hit a pop to short his third time up to finish his initial fantasy camp voyage with a respectable 1–3. I started to feel better about dragging Pete to Lakeland.

The games went late into the night and the setting at historic Henley Field was a pretty one. Night baseball is something the

Pirates don't do, so this was a new experience for me. It had been a long time since I'd played a ball game under the lights, probably dating back to softball games in Miami during the late seventies. Plus, we were able to cap it off with a win. All night I kept thinking of how much I enjoy doing this. Then I wondered if I would feel the same way a day later.

It was posted that we would play three games on Wednesday at ten, two, and six to try and make up the games that were lost. It's one thing to make up the games; it's another to have aging bodies well enough to play. This would be very tough on everyone.

It was late and time to call it a day. Tomorrow's forecast is sunshine and plenty of baseball.

Wednesday

This morning came early in Lakeland after a late Tuesday at the ballpark.

The Tigers trainers wanted to see Pete first thing, so we got to the complex at eight o'clock and Pete went for treatment on the pulled hammy. They iced and rolled it and told him he could play, but cautiously, and encouraged him to use a designated runner. Too bad, because now we couldn't witness how self-professed "quick and fast" he really was.

Three games were on the docket for us. Even Ernie Banks, he of the famed "let's play two," would be impressed that we were scheduled for three.

Unfortunately, Pete couldn't escape the wrath of Judge Warden in kangaroo court. Judge told him, "I understand you made no bones about how quick you are running the bases. Your first at-bat you took two steps out of the box and now you need a walker to get around. At your size you probably only have a little hamstring anyway," so he kept the fine equal to Pete's 5'4" frame and fined him only $2.

Game one of the day followed and the hangover we had from the late game on Tuesday lingered. The Tigers game rules differed somewhat from the Pirates. At both camps, it was a camper that pitched all game, but each pitcher could only pitch three innings in a game. If a Tigers pitcher walks three batters in a row or hits three batters in any inning, he must be removed.

Of course, there is no bunting, stealing, or passed balls at either camp. A Detroit rule I like is no leading off base, because if the ball advances safely to the outfield, everyone is entitled to one base. Too often in Pirates camp, a batter would lace a base hit to the outfield only to have the outfielder force a runner at second or third because no one has the legs to get there in time. The Tigers system rewards base hits and makes teams pay for errors.

Wooden bats only, like in Bradenton, and nine fielders to a squad, but everyone in the lineup hits. If there are twelve active, you bat one through twelve but only nine go onto the field.

Our opponents were a team coached by Warden and former outfielder Johnny Grubb. Before we knew it, we trailed 6–0 going into the bottom of the fifth and final inning, given the shortened inning structure that would allow us to complete all three games today. Our collective alarm went off and twenty minutes later we pushed across seven runs for a very improbable 7–6 win.

I didn't have a good game. I only had two at-bats with a walk and struck out swinging. Gimpy Pete fared much better with a single to center, a walk, and a run scored. Only in fantasy camp can you have a 414 home-run hitter like Darrell Evans come up to namesake Peter Evans, give him a fist bump, and say, "Nice hit!"

A quick lunch hour was followed by the afternoon game against a team coached by Dave Bergman and Jack Billingham. They were also coming off a win in the morning game.

Last year at Pirates camp, I'd played with my circa early sixties model first baseman's glove. It had gotten me through every game in my youth. It turns out I was overly optimistic to think an almost-fifty-year-old glove could make it through fantasy camp. Every game or two, a ball would go completely through the webbing. Much like me, it was getting old and frayed. Fortunately, the Pirates clubhouse guys had a needle and strong thread and I had the cash to tip.

I knew it was silly to keep playing with such a beater, but I couldn't bring myself to retire my childhood glove, nor did I give it much thought when Pirates week ended. Thankfully, longtime business colleague and friend Mike Hallman gave me a brand-spanking-new black Rawlings first baseman's glove for the holidays right before I left for Lakeland, presumably more out of pity than kindness. I never thought that at fifty-eight I would be as excited by a new baseball glove as I was when I was eight. It's a luxury to be able to catch a ball and know it won't pop out the other side. The new mitt was reliable.

In the first inning of today's second game, the first batter hit a ground ball to third. An errant throw to first put me in the position of coming off the base, picking the ball out of the dirt backhanded, and tagging the runner coming by me in one fell swoop. The timing had to be perfect and it was. The new glove did its magic.

Billingham, a 145-major-league-game winner, was coaching first and asked, "Can you do that all the time?" Shhhh. Keep it our secret, please.

The third batter of the inning hit a rope over my head that somehow I was able to leap (as high as I still can go) and snag. Billingham shook his head as I marched off the field to high fives! Then, for good measure, the first out of the second inning also forced me to pick one out of the dirt. This time I was afraid to look at Billingham.

After the inning I had to use the restroom, a wooden outhouse structure located in the middle of the compound with the four ball fields of Tigertown surrounding it. As I tried to exit the bathroom and get back to our game, the door wouldn't open. I pushed, knocked, yelled, and screamed for help. Mysteriously, a large oil drum filled with sand was conveniently put in front of the door. If sly grins were an admissible legal indictment, then Jack Billingham should be doing jail time.

Once I got out of the restroom and back to the field we continued to play well. I walked my first time up and then hit a very solid single to right-center my second time, which forced me to run the bases. No doubt the best part of the game and probably for the whole week was scoring a run on a sacrifice fly after eventually getting to third base. I chugged all the way home from third. I thought I would never get there, but I arrived safely, completely winded and elated. Scoring on a sacrifice fly at fifty-eight years old could be a lifetime highlight!

Though this was one of my best games of the two camps, Pete wasn't as lucky at the plate. He went hitless with a line out to center and struck out swinging. He played a good defensive game at second base and helped us limp home for the 8–5 win and a sweep of the day's first two games.

After a short break, we moved back to historic Henley Field for the evening game, where we played the night before. In the twilight I could see that it was a cute little bandbox of a ballpark. It opened in 1925 as a major league spring training park and seats 1,000 people on metal bleachers. Its claim to fame, other than its age, is that Ty Cobb once played there. Now it can footnote that both Ty Cobb and Roy Berger have played there. It's still a perfect old time baseball movie setting and a special experience, even if it was our third game of the day.

Nighttime baseball is a treat, but tonight just wasn't our night. We played the Bergman-Billingham team again that we had easily handled only a few hours earlier, but it was a completely different game. We were flat, partly because of the spent emotion playing two games already. Then we got word that we had lost three players to injury, including one of our best hitters, forty-year-old Jason Kocembo, who is probably on the DL until next January with a torn ACL.

We went through the motions and were beaten decisively 9–3, leaving us with two wins in three games for the day and an overall record of 3–1 with two games remaining before the playoffs. You know you're playing for better days when you leave your pitcher in to be skewered while trailing 5–3 late in the game. A 5–3 deficit became 9–3 as our guy couldn't find home plate with a telescope. I looked in the dugout at Frank Tanana and he shrugged his shoulders and asked, "What do you want me to do?"

I felt like yelling back, "You're a major league pitcher. Anything you can tell him would be better than nothing," but I decided to stay silent.

He yelled, "Berger, go settle him down." A couple of pitches later, our guy found the strike zone without my help. Changing pitchers certainly would have been a good idea, but we needed fresh arms for tomorrow. We took our lumps and looked forward to a warm shower and bed.

The team may have had a tough game, but I did well with a single to center, an RBI, and a walk. In fact, I had my best at-bat of camp tonight and it came on the walk. I was the third hitter in the first inning against the best pitcher we have seen so far, Brad Walraven, a forty-something-year-old who threw fifty-five to sixty mph, but was extremely crafty with his pitch placement, a camp rarity. I fell behind a ball and two strikes and then drew an eight-pitch walk just trying to foul off anything around the plate. It was one of those walks that when it was finally over really felt earned by fouling pitches off and just trying to stay alive at the plate.

I had a nice surprise during tonight's game. One of my Pirates teammates from last year, Kevin Kubala, the retired Pittsburgh police officer, came over with his wife Barb to see some Tigers fantasy action a few days before the opening of Pirates camp. They live outside of Orlando, so the trip to Lakeland took less than an hour. With rare exception, most of the fantasy camp types tend to lock on to one team and one camp and don't have the opportunity to see another camp in action. While the twilight inhibited a lot of sight-seeing, I was able to run Kevin over to Tigertown after our game ended and gave him the mini-tour. We left our shoes on. He left Lakeland with a much better appreciation for Pirate City and Bradenton.

Curfew came early after a long day, but Pete and I had time to stop in the lounge for a nightcap. My night was made when Walraven, the winning pitcher against us just an hour or so earlier, came over and told me how convinced he was he had me struck out and how pissed off he was that I was able to draw a walk. Walraven is a good pitcher and an even better guy, so I just knew that wouldn't sit well with him. It helped temper the loss.

Thursday

Today was scheduled to be "Moving Day" at Tigertown. The final two games of the regular schedule among the six teams would determine playoff seeds and the all-important first round playoff bye.

Instead, it was "Black and Blue Attrition Day." At this point in the week, and much like Pirates camp, the line in the trainer's room was longer than the line at breakfast. Everyone was feeling the impact of playing four games in less than twenty-four hours and almost everyone showed some noticeable ailment.

At Pirates camp, I spent some time with the trainers, ice, and IcyHot. This year I was on base a lot, did all my own running, and I felt pretty good. As a bonus, I was able to get my legs in and out of bed all by themselves. This morning, however, it took about five minutes per leg for me to get on my uniform pants. My quads were sore, but all in all, I felt better than I ever did at Pirates camp, and I believed I could make it through the week.

Alas, poor Pete didn't fare as well. He had an eight a.m. call to visit the training room to get his hamstring iced and rolled. He limped out about fifteen minutes later and his right hand was bandaged as well. He was hit with a pitch on Wednesday and it had swollen so much the trainers wrapped it with an ACE bandage to keep the swelling down. The guy was a mess.

Kangaroo court followed and I was cited for another fine I really didn't see coming. Judge Warden said, "Berger, when your coach tells you to go settle a pitcher down, it might be a good idea to not wait until he throws fifteen balls in a row, and then he finally throws a strike and gets an out, and then you go talk to him. He doesn't need you anymore." The fine was $2 and I decided to test the appeal process. I told Judge I was appealing because I went over and told our pitcher what a good job he just did. The judge contemplated then immediately denied the appeal, which now cost me $4. As soon as he denied the appeal I told him I wanted to withdraw my appeal. After he finished laughing, he hit me with another $2, upping the total to $6. I'd paid almost as much in fines in three days as I had tuition for this camp.

Finally, it was time to play ball. The weather cooperated and served up a sun-drenched day for our slated doubleheader. We were tied for the best record in camp at 3–1. Our first game was against the other team with the identical record in a game that ultimately would decide the top seed in the playoffs.

We jumped out to a 4–1 lead after three innings and then were victimized by the rule that declares a pitcher can only pitch three innings in a game. Our forty-three-year-old ace Ward Brigham was done, we had no other arms left, and ultimately we slopped our way out of the top seed with a 9–5 spanking to a team coached by a rather subdued Rozema and the very affable Tony Phillips.

I was 1–1 with a single to right and two more walks. I walked a lot this week, but I was waiting for pitches to hit and not swinging just for the sake of swinging. While fully understanding the downside of walking is having to run the bases, I'll take that rather than chase bad stuff. I also made my first fielding error of camp, booting a very playable ground ball. Of course, I blamed it on the new glove.

Pete was hitless in three at-bats because he had trouble gripping the bat with his bandaged hand. Of greater concern, he aggravated the hammy again by stretching for a ball at second base and went down, or in baseball parlance, he was "snipered." The trainer came out and helped him off the field since someone else on another field was using Pete's walker.

The main event for most of the campers followed lunch, which was a half-hour long question-and-answer session with Hall of Famer Al Kaline, stationed right outside the clubhouse. Kaline to a Tigers fan is what Willie Mays would be to a Giants fan, or what Mickey Mantle would be to Yankees fan, or for me what it would be like to listen to Roberto Clemente. Kaline is now seventy-five years old and still very recognizable with a headful of silver hair that gives him a debonair appearance. He was incredibly engaging and interesting and I could have listened for hours to the old stories he told.

Unfortunately, we didn't have the time. We knew we had to win our afternoon game to clinch the second playoff seed. Most importantly, to win our next game meant we wouldn't have to report early on Friday for a first round playoff game. This proved to be great motivation for everyone.

We were able to pitch Brigham for three innings and we gave him plenty of run support. We pounded our way to a 10–2 win over the team coached by Dan Petry and Larry Herndon. Petry, a 125-game winner in the bigs for Detroit, California, Atlanta, and Boston has been on cloud nine all week as his son Jeff had been called up to play for the Edmonton Oilers in the NHL.

The game was close for a while, but we broke it open during the middle innings and coasted to the second seed in the playoff round. I had a good game and went 2–3 with a solid single to center and then a rope to right with the bases loaded that knocked in two runs. After my single to center, I went back out to first base only to have Larry Herndon, a lifetime .274 major league hitter with 1,300 career hits and 107 home runs say to me, "Nice poke." Once again, I was reminded of what a wonderful world this is.

Pete was wrapped like a mummy but played the entire game in right field since we were getting pretty thin on our roster. He went 1–3 with a single to left and a very timely RBI.

The win secured the first round bye, but we lost even more players to injuries, and to top it off, Friday's forecast was for more storms.

That evening the Tigers brass tried their best to keep us entertained during what was becoming a very long week. They encouraged us to come back to the Lakeland Inn lounge after dinner for a comedy show to keep our minds off our bodies and the lousy weather. It was a valiant attempt.

The opening act was one of the campers, sixty-three-year-old Mark Brier, who ironically also hails from East Meadow, New

York, where he still calls home. Mark has attended Tigers camp regularly for the past ten years as a Tigers fan from his youth. He's a food industry exec in real life, but also dabbles in stand-up comedy. I can identify with him. I fooled around with it too, back in 2007, when I took a class for six weeks in Atlanta, a 300-mile round trip from my home in Birmingham. I actually made eight appearances on stages in both Atlanta and Birmingham. One performance was great, a couple were good, a few more were mediocre, and one absolutely bombed, which prompted me to think about the sanctity of chasing a fifty-five mph fastball at fantasy baseball camp.

Brier still does his gig, mainly for senior citizens at public libraries. His business card reads, "Comedian and Utility Infielder." His stuff is borscht-belt vaudevillian and mainly for the octogenarian Jewish crowd. Considering he and I were the only two Jews in the Lakeland Room, the upside for serious laughs was a long shot.

Jon Warden followed and Warden is a funny guy. After his career in baseball ended, he did some TV work and was a regular comedy guest on ESPN's *Cold Pizza* and performed in clubs around the country. Warden, as kangaroo court judge, had a huge advantage as he has been proven to be funny. Only at a baseball fantasy camp could you get away with your thirty-minute stand-up set consisting mainly of one-liners about your prostate. Warden did.

Friday

In baseball parlance, it's said that a batter gets a "haircut" when the opposing pitcher throws a high, hard one near the hitter's head. In Detroit Tigers fantasy camp jargon, it's something to do when your entire fantasy baseball day gets washed out once again by rain.

Torrential storms overnight on Thursday combined with a steady rain on Friday, which made the fields unplayable for our final day of competition, playoff day. A decision was made before nine a.m. that for the third time in five days we were rained out. This was not exactly what we signed up for, but it was something we were getting used to and there were no alternatives other than to just find a way to pass the day.

The playoff schedule was moved to Saturday, which was forecast to be chilly and clear. Not only is there nothing for us to do today, as we exhausted all the "rain day" alternative activities, we also lost the Legends game against the former Tiger ballplayers on Saturday in exchange for the playoff round. From my memories of my Pirates experience, the Legends game was a fun day that I probably looked at differently because it was the culmination of a full week. The Legends game is only two innings, so if that's all we have left in this camp it would be fitting as a total wash-out week. We thought the mantra of "start slow and taper off" would be in reference to our bodies and health, not our camp experience.

Through life you learn to make the best of things you can't control, be it weather or flight delays or business or life situations that for whatever reason don't turn out the way you might envision. I've been through a painful divorce and a job or two that didn't work out and I've learned to get through it and move ahead. Certainly a rainy week playing baseball doesn't resonate as long and deeply as a failed marriage or a job gone awry, but with age we learn to cope with things both big and small and push on.

So we made the best of things and today I got a haircut, literally, and didn't have to duck away from the high, hard one as the weather was too lousy for anyone to be pitching. On the other hand, maybe Pete took a high, hard one this week or was just getting woozy from the inactivity. He said he needed to find an ATM. He was driving. Next thing I know he's making a left into a blood bank. I said, "Where are you going?" Pete replied, "Into this bank to find an ATM." I told him he might want to find one that specializes in green withdrawals, not red donations.

Because of the weather, our team spent a lot of time together away from the ball field. We spent hours at the hotel and in the clubhouse sitting around talking and getting to know each other and our businesses. We went out to dinner as a large group a couple of times and even found a wine bar or two in Lakeland. Our team was an interesting collection of fifteen from all across the country. Incredibly, those from Michigan, naturally a stronghold state for Tiger fans and campers, were in the minority. We had six from Michigan, three from Florida, and singles from Alabama, Texas, Connecticut, New Jersey, North Carolina, and Arizona. We were restaurant managers, insurance types, aviation experts, healthcare professionals, actuaries, a chef, landscape architects, one in the social media industry, a training specialist for the US Army, and even a farmer. We were an incredible melting pot of talent and professions who left our lives behind for a week to live a fantasy. Now we'd have to see how far that bonding will carry in Saturday's playoff round.

I know I jabbed at Pete a lot during the week, but I really have a lot of respect and admiration for him. Not only did he agree to do this, which many, many others wouldn't, but despite being banged up he always had a great attitude and wanted to contribute as much as he could to the team. He had four hits in fourteen at-bats for a .285 average with a walk and an RBI. It was incredible that he could hold a bat or get any leverage off his injured leg in his rookie try. He never complained once, did the very best he could on the field, and was the type of teammate everyone gravitated to. For Pete's sake, I kept the blood bank story between us, until now. I was really proud of the guy in spite of the week I subjected him to.

Now another strong Friday afternoon thunderstorm makes Saturday iffy as well. The entire weather-delayed week started slow and really was tapering off. We had better play tomorrow. I have no more hair to cut.

Saturday

Late Friday, we were told the Legends game today against the pro staff was canceled but at least we could save our playoff round. After another late Friday night/early Saturday morning rain, we awoke to learn we were going to play the Legends game after all, but had lost the playoff round.

Nobody understood this decision. The Tigertown fields were deemed unplayable but the main stadium, Joker Marchant, was in good enough shape, so the Legends game was back on. Scrapping the playoff round to play an inning or two against the big guys didn't really create any enthusiasm among the camp. The revised schedule shortened us about eight innings of regulation play and now the two playoff games were gone as well. With the playoffs scrapped, we had lost over three full games during this rain-plagued week. That's a lot of baseball to lose when you only do it one week a year and have paid a nice price for the privilege.

So we reported to Joker Marchant for the Legends game, which would wrap up our playing week with only the closing banquet to follow tonight. Joker Marchant is a pretty ballpark with a major league feel. It was built in 1966 and holds 9,000 people. The real Tigers play their spring training slate in this park and it's a spring stadium name familiar to most baseball fans.

Pre-game, all campers were introduced by name and hometown for the ceremonial trot out to the baseline by Tiger broadcaster Jim Price. Following the camper intros, the Tiger pro staff supplying the opposition trotted out. There was Willie Horton, Dave Bergman, Dave Rozema, Frank Tanana, Tony Phillips, Jack Billingham, Darrell Evans, John Hiller, Milt Wilcox, Ike Blessitt, Jon Warden, Larry Herndon, and John Grubb. Hiller and Wilcox were there early for the second week of the back-to-back camps and Blessitt recovered enough from his bug to be able to play. We still aren't certain if he got his funding or not.

Each team played a two-inning game against the Legends in the order we finished in round robin play. With no playoffs to settle the issue, our team finished second with a record of four up and two down, one half game behind the declared winners at 4–1–1. It was my second runner-up finish in as many camps.

A crowd settled in to watch the action with only about 8,980 good seats still available.

We were the second game of the morning. It was a chilly day; the high was about sixty degrees. The wind was blowing, the sun was shining, and all we wanted to do on getaway day was play ball.

Our spot in the sun came quickly, and our coach Frank Tanana chose to throw against us. Frank was known for throwing ninety mph in the 1970s and seventy mph in the 1990s, or so the lore goes. He tossed at about sixty this morning.

During my at-bat I worked him to a two ball, two strike count and then clearly Daiquiri had a flashback.

He stepped off the mound and contemplated. As one of only two pitchers in major league history to give up home runs to Aaron and Bonds, he surely had no desire to add my name to the list.

He threw me an inside fastball that sawed the bat into pieces. Most of the bat went further than the ball and by the time everyone ducked for cover, the ball had settled on the right side of the infield for a cheap, broken bat hit. In the box score, it was as good as a solid shot to right. I'm now 1–2 lifetime against big league pitching. Zane Smith last year in Pirates camp was the only one that could handle me.

I made it around to third base by the time Pete batted. He grabbed a stick, left his multiple ailments in the dugout, and was ready to take a shot against Tanana.

On the third pitch, Pete hit a ground ball to Darrell Evans at third, who tossed him out at first but not before Pete got credit for an RBI as I headed home safely.

Our inning in the field was good. Pete had two putouts on a pop fly and ground ball. Our shortstop decided to test me one more time by throwing a ball from deep short that I had to pick out of the dirt. When I finally opened my eyes, the ball rested comfortably in my new glove, which, by the way, I love again.

I played way over my head this week. Despite having less active playing time than I had hoped, my statistics were surprisingly strong. I hit .667 with six hits in nine times at-bat, six walks, and three RBIs.

Even better, I also had legs under me all week, a big change from not being able to get in or out of bed last year with the Pirates. For being one of the older campers this week, I was very pleased with my defense. I had perhaps the best defensive half inning of my life on Wednesday, which Jack Billingham took none too kindly.

The on-field memory and highlight for me was defying the laws of aging and physics by scoring on a sacrifice fly. Seemed like I'd never get there, but I huffed and puffed and finally blew my way across for a run. When I caught my breath twenty minutes later, it sure felt good.

We also were lucky and played on a team of really great guys among a camp that featured quality people. Rookies were made to feel like ten-year veterans and nobody was a stranger.

But when you've had enough, you've had enough. We finished the Legends game about eleven a.m. and the only thing remaining on the camp agenda was the closing banquet at six p.m., meaning another six or seven idle hours in the vanilla confines of the dreary Lakeland Inn. Pete and I looked at each other and we both knew what we wanted. We quickly said good-bye to our teammates, hustled off to the locker room to grab our stuff, and didn't really care if Ghost saw us with our shoes on or not. We knew it was time to go home.

We jumped in the car and headed to Orlando. En route, we called the airlines and we were able to rebook our flights for later that day as opposed to waiting until the next morning to leave. We felt like we'd just won the playoffs.

Sure, the week was weather-marred, but as the old story goes, a lousy day on the golf course beats a good day in the office. It's the same for a week playing baseball, and it was a bonus having Pete along, who was the first to laugh at himself and seemed to enjoy it all.

I've said that Pittsburgh puts a bad product on the field during the major league season, but I can't believe anyone runs a fantasy camp as well as they do. Now I'm sure of it.

The Detroit experience was good, but a very distant second to the Pirates. No doubt the weather literally dampened part of it, but Pittsburgh ran a tighter, more professional, and organized operation that left the camper truly feeling they were given a major league experience.

Despite that, when I got home Andi asked me if the week was worth it. Absolutely! I got to play ball with ninety other aging, balding, paunchy, and clearly on the back nine of life "kids." I got to walk around for a week wearing a baseball uniform. At my age, that truly is a priceless experience.

Catching my breath after rumbling home on a sac fly.

Pete asks Frank Tanana (l) and Darrell Evans (r) to pick on someone their own size.

The dean of kangaroo court judges, Jon Warden, levies more fines.

Pete puts his bumps and bruises aside and takes a cut.

Fifth Inning

Pinstripes

January 2012

7 woke up this morning and for a minute, I thought it was July 1, 1966. Or perhaps July 1, 1967. Or maybe July 1, 1968, or 1969. It could even have been January 15, 2011.

On those July dates from 1966 to 1969, I arose and the feeling was unmistakable: *Camp begins today.*

Back in the 1960s, my parents sent me and my two brothers during July and August to an outpost in Woodbourne, New York, two hours from our Long Island home. We called it "sleep-away" camp, and we were sent allegedly for our own enjoyment, until we became parents ourselves and discovered who really got the two-month break.

Camp Impala was small, about 100 kids, who ranged in age from seven to sixteen. It set my folks back a pretty penny, too— about $500 for the summer per kid. Not $500 a week. Five hundred dollars for the entire eight weeks. Even in 2013 dollars, it's pretty incredible what $65 a week got back in the sixties: room, board, food, and enough incredible memories to last a lifetime.

The first summer I was ticketed for an eight-week deployment was in 1965. I woke up that July morning and had no idea what I was in for. I felt anxiety, trepidation, and fear. By the following summer, all those fears had been pushed aside by sheer anticipation of what lies ahead.

How soon does the bus leave? Please let these next eight weeks go slowly. Very slowly.

The experience and excitement compounded from summer to summer until finally, at the age of seventeen in August 1969, I concluded my five-year run at Camp Impala as a senior counselor and ultimately Color War General, the highest honor that can be bestowed at camp. I also was the stud first baseman on the inter-camp softball team. It's still the only time I've been a stud at anything.

Those summers still resonate today. I've been reunited over the past five years with a dozen or so Impala alums, many of whom I still see on a regular basis on my travels around the country. And the names we had for each other back then—Buzzy, Scooter, Duke (I was Bronco)—still stick.

For some guys, hunting is their thing. Others guys fish. Golf holds interest to me, but I need the sun shining, the weather warm, and a good, long-lasting cigar for the back nine. Gambling once had its appeal but has since waned.

When I decided to be a kid again two years ago and headed off to Pirates camp, I woke up with the same feeling I had in 1965: how did I get into this and how do I get out of it? Fantasy baseball camp, long an unrealized dream for me, beckoned. My wife said I had to go because she knew it was something I wanted to do and would really enjoy. I wasn't sure what was ahead, but I signed up anyway. I got up that morning looking for a way out.

The Tigers experience last year wasn't as good as the Pirates, but in fairness it never had a chance. Even though I'd brought along my friend Pete for companionship, rain virtually every day shortened the ball playing and made some days really, really long. I found "old-guy" baseball to be the one week a year I really look forward to. The feeling of walking around all day in a baseball uniform with my BlackBerry (yes, I'm still one of those guys) and the rest of my adult life left behind in a locker in the clubhouse is indescribable. It truly has become the most wonderful week of the year.

The first two fantasy camp experiences whet my appetite for this year. My youthful devotion to the Pirates that was born in 1960 through my dad and reached its peak from 1964 to 1967 dissolved through my teen years to a passing fancy. In 1976, I became a devout Yankees fan, a team I truly despised in the sixties.

One afternoon in March 1976, I was sitting at my desk as Public Relations/Media Director at the Hollywood Greyhound Track, my second job out of college. We often had ballplayers and celebrities visit Hollywood during our racing season. The track was fun and close enough to the spring training camps to make it an easy drive for many of the players. The seventies Yankees trained in nearby Fort Lauderdale. Most of them would just show up at Hollywood and expect to be taken care of. In those days, with games mainly played during the day, a dining room table at Hollywood during high season became a pretty tough ticket.

I got a call from the Yankees PR department. They wanted to know if I could make arrangements for Thurman Munson and his wife to have dinner at the track. Thurman Munson? The Yankees captain? Calling me, a twenty-three-year-old, to get a table for the Yankees captain? How good was this? I took the liberty of telling the Yankees PR flak that of course Mr. Munson would be taken care of, and pressed my luck a bit further by telling him to have the captain look me up when he arrived.

A couple of hours passed and the track receptionist phoned me, "There is a Mr. Monster here to see you." With that intro, I figured it was either Herman Munster or Thurman Munson; it didn't matter which. I almost leapt over my desk to get out to the reception area. There stood the Yankees captain with his very attractive wife, Diana. Thurman Munson, with his curly hair, bushy moustache, and squat yet muscular physique. Thurman had a reputation of being gruff with the media, and that personality transcended to the public as a bit of a badass type of character. It turns out nothing could have been further from the truth.

Munson was a true gentleman, as warm, caring, and personable as one could be with the public every time he came to the track, which ended up being often. Only from that night on, he phoned me directly.

Our relationship continued over the next three springs, and on nights when Diana was tending to their kids, Thurm would bring some of his teammates along to have dinner and bet the races. In fact, he was so enamored with the racing business that we spoke about putting an investor group together to buy a racetrack that was on the market in New England. It became personal and my deep affection for the Yankees was born.

I went to Boston over Labor Day weekend in 1978 to visit my friend Greg Farley, a racing writer for the Boston Herald-American. Greg had tickets to the Saturday Yankees-Red Sox game at Fenway. The Yankees came into that series trailing Boston by four games and proceeded to sweep the weekend. Only six weeks earlier, the Yankees were fourteen games behind in the American League East pennant race. The Yankees, in a weekend known forever as the Boston Massacre, won the four games by a combined 42–9. That sweep was the catalyst to one of the biggest collapses in baseball history as the Bombers ultimately won the AL East championship in a one-game playoff against Boston propelled by Bucky Dent's home run off Mike Torrez. Then they advanced to win the ALCS over Kansas City and beat the Dodgers in the World Series.

No matter which of our sides won, Greg and I planned to take in the greyhound races that evening after the game at Wonderland Park in nearby Revere, Massachusetts. As we walked into the track dining room, someone shouted, "Roy! What are you doing here? Come sit with us." It was Munson at a table along with teammates Ron Guidry (who threw the shutout that day), Lou Piniella, Mickey Rivers, Goose Goosage, Catfish Hunter, and Craig Nettles...all Yankees stars.

It was an overwhelming experience to spend part of the night with these guys. Talk about being out of my league! They were throwing $50s and $100s on the table, betting like money was no object, and truly enjoying the first three days of what ultimately would be the four-game sweep. It's a memory of a lifetime to have experienced how much fun they were having with the baseball world clearly tipping in their favor.

Ironically, I became the general manager of that very facility, Wonderland Park, eleven years later in 1989. I still hated the home team.

My relationship with Thurman Munson ended tragically on August 2, 1979, when he perished at age thirty-two in an airplane he was piloting in his hometown of Canton, Ohio. Nothing was more important to him than family. Diana and the children stayed in Canton while Thurman played baseball halfway across the country. He found the most expedient way to get between home and work was with his own airplane. A pilot's license soon followed, and on some days after the Yankees played an afternoon game, Thurman would start the engines and spend the night in Canton before heading back to New York, or wherever the Yankees were playing the next day.

The only positive of that very dark August day was that Thurman Munson died doing what he wanted to do, in a place he so longingly wanted to be. I was spending that summer of 1979 helping to manage a racetrack in Plainfield, Connecticut, and remember hearing the news like it was yesterday. It took a while for me to compose myself. I had a colleague by the name of Aaron Silver, who was a regular at the track and close friends with Lou Piniella, one of Munson's best pals. Aaron phoned and asked me if I wanted to go to Thurman's funeral with him. He had a private plane, so we left from Hartford on the morning of August 6 and joined the chaotic, numbing scene in Canton.

Two Kodak moments remain forever: Yankees manager Billy Martin bawling uncontrollably and having to be steadied and escorted by his coaches, and Thurman's four-year-old son Michael dressed in his Yankees pinstripes with the number 15. I still get the shakes thinking about it.

That night, a group of us were in Yankee Stadium as the Yankees returned from the funeral in Canton to play a game no one had any interest in playing. Baltimore was the opponent and the Yankees took the field with only eight players. The catcher's position remained vacant as the crowd stood for what seemed like an hour and just applauded the memory of the Yankees captain no longer with us. It was chilling.

Since that day, I have been a die-hard Yankees fan. In fact, there are only two teams in baseball I follow and root for: the Yankees, and whomever is playing Boston.

So, after two experiences playing real fantasy baseball—one good and one wet—and the legs and other body parts seemingly still in place, I decided this was the year to become a Yankee in Tampa. In typical Yankees fashion, the cost of the week is about 25 percent higher than both Pittsburgh and Detroit; but hey, it's the Yankees. What do you expect?

The question I received more than any other in advance of this year's camp was, "Is Pete going with you?" Pete Evans, a business colleague from Connecticut, wanted to go to Tigers camp not necessarily because he is a baseball buff, but because "I wanted to spend the week with you. Sounds like fun." I've gotten to the point in life where nobody really wants to spend much time with me, save perhaps for Andi (sometimes), and always for the three-year-old crush of my life, the chow/retriever rescue mix we call Ibis.

So where's Pete this year? Who knows? He had enough last year and with his hamstring and hand now fully healed, he no doubt opted for a Maker's Mark on the veranda to watch the sailboats pass as opposed to the pre-game morning stretch.

Meet Barry Otelsberg: a sixty-one-year-old retired successful Southern California banking executive and my friend since 1965.

Barry's family owned Camp Impala. The Os (we will drop the "Otelsberg" from here forward, as they were always the "Os," not "Otelsbergs") were the complete camp family. Grandma Claire and Grandpa Harry were not only the owners, but were the matriarch and patriarch of camp; Mom LilaO was our head counselor, brother JerryO and sisters BarbaraO and LoriO were camp mainstays. Their dad, MartyO, was a weekend presence when not managing rock 'n' roll stars during the week. The family was raised in Brooklyn before relocating west in the late 1960s.

Truth be told, BarryO is two years older than me, a generation at summer camp. Our acquaintance spanned two months every year. Barry was smart back then and still is today. He knew the way to the ladies' hearts was through horses, and Barry managed the camp stable. Eight horses and all the young cowgirls he wanted. He finally roped the gal of his dreams thirty-five years ago, Joan, and they live happily ever after right outside of Los Angeles. They have their hands full with seven daughters. Yep, seven—and as a bonus, six grandchildren and one great-grandbaby. That also adds up to seven; the same number BarryO will wear on his Yankees uniform this week.

We spent five summers together from 1965 to 1969 and then lost touch until 2007 when his sister, BarbaraO, tried to reunite as many Camp Impala alums as she could find. Some thirty-eight years later, seventy of us spent a great weekend in upstate New York like it was 1969 again.

Barry and I were in touch sporadically over the five years until last January when Tigers camp ended, and Barry sent me a note that read, "If you want to do the Yankees next year, I'm interested in going with you." Barry cautioned that he had no idea if he could even swing a bat, never mind hit a ball, and before committing, he wanted to give it a try. On the evening of January 24, 2011, I got this late-night e-mail from Barry:

"I just got back from the batting cage and I'M IN! I did better than I expected. I only whiffed on four of the forty balls. I also realized that I have never played baseball before, only softball. I haven't been this excited since I was twelve years old!"

I didn't want to temper his excitement. At our age, any excitement is very, very good. When he found out we were going to be Yankees for the week, the roof couldn't contain him. Barry has been a lifelong, devout Yankees fan. In early June, I sent him the DVD of the Detroit fantasy camp. Then came the doubts. He wrote, "As I was watching it I kept saying to myself, 'What have I done?' I don't know if I can play. Too late now. I am in with both feet."

You've gotta love this guy. He never played a lick of competitive baseball in his life and was willing to put his money where his mouth was and give it a whirl. As much as I love the camp experience, the excitement of this sixty-one-year-old who has never played hardball and was this enthused gave me all the impetus I needed.

I gave him some pre-camp advice. Unlike Pete, he listened. I told Barry that stretching is key, and if he could find a baseball coach or even a high school program where he could do some fielding and hitting just as a precursor for the week, it would go a long way.

Just as he promised, Barry indeed jumped in with both feet. Barry's feet just aren't that big. He stands 5'6", 145 pounds, but he towers over Pete's comparatively small frame of 5'4". I think the problem is mine. At 6'3", there must be something about traveling with these shorter boys that gives me some sense of security.

Before I knew it, Barry was a regular at yoga class and found a coach who worked with him twice a week; fielding one day and the other spent in the batting cage. Everything was going great. Barry's excitement level became that of the twelve-year-old, until a few weeks went by without hearing a word from my future campmate. I reached out to see how training was going. "Not so good, Bronco," Barry moaned through the phone. "I've been in bed for three days and still can't move." It seems a sciatic nerve compression felled my to-be New York Yankees teammate and it wasn't the first time for Barry, either. Surgery many years ago corrected the first bout of the occurrence. He said he hoped to be out of bed in a day or two and was optimistic he could resume some type of physical activity. I cautioned him that fantasy baseball camp was not worth permanent injury, and another Yankees camp would be waiting for him once he felt better.

He understood, but he didn't want to toss in the towel and became more determined than ever. A week went by, and then he felt ready to go back to yoga and take a few swings in the cage. All went well until he found himself bedridden again. I started to look for Pete's number, who was looking like a fine physical specimen compared to Barry.

He said, "I'm going to be there and play. I'm coming." His plane from LA landed in Tampa at 5:45 p.m. Sunday. He walked off the plane unaided.

Monday

We spent Monday morning at an optional conditioning session in Clearwater, about thirty minutes from our base in Tampa. It was held at the old springtime headquarters of the Philadelphia Phillies and about twenty-three Yankees fantasy campers coughed up $80 for the three-hour workout. It was a really good class of stretching, running, hitting, and defense, and we were both glad we did it. The best part was that Barry competed and got through the three-hour session with minimal pain. In fact, his right leg walked off the field the same time as the rest of his body.

This was actually the second Yankees camp of the very young calendar year. The weekend prior to our arrival, the Yankees hosted 100 ladies at their sold-out women's three-day camp. The boys come in for a week in January and again in November to round out the annual three-camp schedule.

Tonight was the opening banquet when the ninety-five of us would meet the Yankees legends who would be our coaches. The legends list was impressive. On hand were former Yankee greats and notables Al Downing, Bucky Dent, David "Boomer" Wells, Homer Bush, Jake Gibbs, Jeff Nelson, Luis "El Tiante" Tiant, Mickey Rivers, Mike Torrez, Oscar Gamble, Tanyon Sturtze, Ron Blomberg, Roy White, Chris Chambliss, Paul Blair, and Orlando "El Duque" Hernandez. There was no sign of Neil Allen. For a minute, it felt like crashing a private party before Old Timers' Day at Yankee Stadium. It was a truly stellar list and almost all of them were there the weekend before to give the gals a coaching assist, too.

When you are a devout fan of a team, most of the guys are immediately recognizable, such as Wells, Chambliss, Tiant, Rivers, and White, and others suddenly come back into view like you are looking at their Topps rookie card. For me it was that way with the Pirates, but not with the Tigers as I never formed an affinity to them.

There was one guy hanging around the hotel lobby, wearing a tattered shirt, a CBS Sports hat, shorts, sandals, and a Diet Coke in his hand. He looked like the rest of us schlubs who came to camp for some self-inflicted pain. Then he was introduced at the evening banquet. He was the designated Hebrew, Ron Blomberg, now sixty-three, who became the first designated hitter in big league baseball history on April 6, 1973, at Fenway Park. And who did he face for that historical at-bat? Another one in camp this week, Luis Tiant, was on the hill for Boston and let Blomberg be remembered forever with a bases-loaded walk. The bat he brought to the plate, but never used, is encased in Cooperstown. *Designated Hebrew* became the designated hitter's 2006 book title. Blomberg is a nice guy willing to have a conversation with anyone who had time.

Teams were unveiled and Barry and I will be coached by Homer Bush and Oscar Gamble on a team named, appropriately enough, The Pinstripes. Barry and I laughed so hard we were on the verge of tears—we decided just the night before that Bush and Gamble were the only two Yanks that didn't excite us, so it only makes sense that we'll have to spend the week with them.

Gamble had a long major league career that spanned seventeen seasons with seven of them as a Yankee. The sixty-three-year-old former outfielder hit 200 career home runs and knocked in 666 runs. He may be best known, however, for having what was arguably the number one, all-time Afro hairdo in major league history. Now, like many of us, he's bald. Gamble is virtually a neighbor of mine who lives in Montgomery, Alabama. He's retired and works with underprivileged kids in their baseball programs.

Bush, a former second baseman and shortstop, played seven seasons in the bigs and part of three years with the Yankees in 1997, 1998, and again in 2004. At thirty-nine years old, he's still young and hit .348 in pinstripes and was a member of the 1998 Yankees World Championship team. In 1999, he was part of the Roger Clemens trade to Toronto that brought Clemens to the Yankees for his great run. Bush's heyday in the bigs was with Toronto in the early 2000s, which was part of my problem. The day-to-day fan interest I had back in the sixties and seventies waned with time and Homer was more a baseball present-day contemporary than the others, who were truly legends from back in my day.

Bush sat at our table at the opening night banquet and was an absolute delight. We might have gotten the short end of a "legend," but I could tell he would be the clubhouse leader in personality. He lives in Dallas and works in the financial services industry. He is personable, engaging, and has a body that still looks like it can easily go nine innings.

The banquet was held in the convention area of the host hotel, the Sheraton Suites, and included a nice video presentation of career highlights of all the Yankee legends in camp. It probably was tough for anyone trying to sleep in the hotel as the noise level hit max with cheers erupting when the Bucky Dent and Chris Chambliss walk-off post season home runs and the David Wells perfect game were shown.

Things start for real tomorrow. We are to report to George M. Steinbrenner Field at seven thirty a.m., where our pinstripes await in the Yankees clubhouse which will be ours for the week. A pair of nine-inning doubleheaders will follow at ten a.m. and two p.m. That's a lot of innings to play at any age, and with the average camper about fifty-five years old, it will take its toll very early in the week. While I'm really worried about Barry's leg and back, he's not, which is good.

I couldn't help but be reminded of the Detroit camp mantra from last year "start slow and taper off."

We may not have much choice.

Tuesday

A day that started with such promise before the sun rose ended in disappointment later that afternoon.

We left the hotel in darkness before seven a.m. so we could be early for our report time to Steinbrenner Field. I had rented a car since we were only a ten-minute drive away and could forego the shuttle bus that ran from the hotel to the field. On our drive, Barry admitted that he was nervous. "It's a good nervous," he said. "I feel like I'm fifteen years old today."

We arrived at the gorgeous Steinbrenner complex the Yankees have called their spring home since 1996, and entered through the main entrance after showing our Yankees ID badge to the receptionist. We were directed through a door behind the reception area and into a hallway that doesn't see the light of day for the public. About fifty yards away was another door marked "Yankees Personnel Only," with our badge the key to admittance to the forbidden territory. Now we were inside the outer clubhouse, with pictures of great Yankees and great Yankees' moments lining both sides of the hallway. The trainers' room was to the left, still unoccupied. I knew that would soon change.

As we approached the clubhouse door, the Yankees pictures on the wall turned into those of Hall of Famers. We excitedly entered the enormous Yankees spring clubhouse, much larger than the Pirates', with the famous Yankee Stadium bunting and frieze lining the ceiling.

We found our team area toward the rear. Waiting for us in our Yankees-inscribed nameplate locker was the culmination of any Yankees fan's fantasy—our pinstripes. Mine was #56 with a matching blue away jersey, as well. Barry had one of the multiple #7s for the week. Also neatly hanging with our uniform tops was a pair of pinstriped baseball pants, a blue warm-up jacket, a blue undershirt, game socks, and for later in the day, Nike sandals and a tote bag so guys like me can carry necessities to the field and not have to use a plastic hotel laundry bag.

What a wonderful, exciting, and memorable moment it was to don the white pinstripes and make sure it was sized properly. Barry was #7 for his baseball hero Mickey Mantle, and I wore #56 again. I couldn't bring myself to smear the memory of my favorite Yankee, Munson, by wearing #15. Plus, I now join the list of Yankees greats who have worn #56, household names: Bill Castro, Andy Cook, Curt Brown, John Cumberland, Brian Dorsett, Rick Down, and Darrell Einertson. Probably the most famous (or infamous) #56 on the Yankees was pitcher-turned-author Jim Bouton, who crossed the line in the late 1960s with his clubhouse tell-all book *Ball Four*.

Today's Yankee #56 is bench coach Tony Pena and the only other one at camp wearing #56 is former Yankees pitcher and now fantasy camp coach Tanyon Sturtze, who wore the number for real from 2004 to 2006.

Of course, the Yankees don't put names on the back of their jerseys because, well, they are the Yankees. The Red Sox don't have names on their home shirts either, as seemingly, the townies know their cavalry, but do help the road fans with names on the away uniforms.

We dressed and exited the clubhouse, made a right turn through the tunnel, and walked under a hanging banner with the famed Joe DiMaggio quote, "I'd like to thank the good Lord for making me a Yankee," and onto the stunning expanse of Steinbrenner Field. It was green, huge, and overwhelming. By the time we caught our breath, it was time to have our pictures taken on the field, at which time I was admonished by the camp photographer that beards are not approved attire for a Yankee. Actually, I was aware of this rule, but never gave it a thought and my razor was back in Birmingham.

Cameos concluded and facial hair still in tow, we made it to breakfast in a nearby pavilion used for group events year round. Barry and I sat with two gents from Sydney, Australia, who had decided a baseball fantasy camp, despite baseball being a very minor sport in Australia, was something they had to do. They were Yankees fans because of the success of former Yankees pitcher Graeme Lloyd, who is an Aussie. If they have bucket lists in Australia, then Yankees camp was on it for these two very nice blokes.

I prepared for this year's camp a bit differently than the last two. For the Pirates and Tigers experiences, I went to a local batting cage about six weeks before having to report to Florida. I would go once a week for about thirty minutes and hit baseballs. I did no throwing or fielding.

This time around, I found a baseball academy a few miles from home and worked directly with the owner, Jarrod Patterson, a former major leaguer. JP, thirty-nine, had lunch in the bigs and played twenty-six games split between Detroit and Kansas City from 2001 to 2003. He was a first and third baseman, hit .238, and poked two home runs. JP is not headed to Cooperstown.

We worked once a week in his baseball-converted warehouse on throwing and fielding and then did some live batting practice, which I really loved. I fully understood that my skill set, or lack thereof, wasn't going to improve, but it was a good workout; I got a good schvitz and hopefully will be a little better off than the guys who did no training at all for this week. I was JP's oldest student by thirty-seven years.

My goal the first time I did this with the Pirates two years ago was to be competitive and get a base hit at some point during the week. Last year with Detroit, I knew I could compete, so I wanted to have fun and enjoy the outing with Pete. This year I'm excited to play with Barry; I hope he can hold up for the week because off the field should be a lot of fun.

My on the field goal this week is an extra base hit. I've never had one. I'm not greedy, I only want one.

I came close to getting an extra base hit in 2010 in Bradenton when I hit a windblown ball over the right fielder's head, but by the time I reached first, my legs started to give out and I couldn't find a lift to take me to second. I just turned around and enjoyed my single. Thirteen other singles have followed. Between the extra training and my added confidence, it's time to take that blazing speed, make a wide turn, and get at least a double on my résumé. I'm afraid a triple is physiologically impossible.

Finally, after all the pomp and circumstance of the last two days, it was time to actually play baseball with a pair of nine-inning doubleheaders on the slate. Nine innings is a lot of old-guy baseball. We headed to Himes Development Center, a training ground for minor league Yankees a couple of miles from the Steinbrenner complex that sits in the imposing shadow of Raymond James Stadium where the NFL Tampa Bay Bucs call home. This morning we play against a team coached by Al Downing and Jake Gibbs, two of the relatively older "legends" who actually made up the Yankees battery for three years in the sixties.

The Yankees play with a couple of different game rules than the Pirates and Tigers. Each team has a minor league instructor assigned to them; young guys who just missed making it in the big leagues and now were working on up-and-coming coaching careers. It was those staffers who pitched the first six innings of each game with the intent to keep the ball in play, as opposed to the other camps that used campers on the mound. In this camp, campers pitch only the last three innings. Quality umpiring keeps things very aboveboard and made the pitchers work for strikes with a fairly consistent speed of about sixty mph, something you didn't see at the other camps when pitchers were, at times, all over the place. The Yankees also use four outfielders, and while very softballish in nature, it did serve its purpose to help move nine-inning games along just a little quicker. Unless of course you lose a base hit to the extra fielder, and then it becomes a downright shitty rule.

Before we knew it, we trailed 8–0 in the opener after two innings. However, as I learned at Pirates camp, a good defense is just as important, if not more so, as a good offense. They got eight runs off of us early, but that was all they were going to score. We chipped away and actually drew within one run to 8–7 in the bottom of the ninth when we had the bases loaded and nobody out. Sadly, we couldn't get the tying run across and the game ended on a very bizarre infield-fly-rule double play featuring Barry right in the middle of what resembled an outtake from a Three Stooges movie with everyone running in different directions. In spite of that, we actually felt good about ourselves coming from that far back early and giving ourselves a chance to win.

My day as a Yankee didn't start very well. My first time at-bat wearing the holy grail of pinstripes, I knew what A-Rod feels like in October. I grounded into my first ever 5–4–3 double play. This humiliating start to my Yankees career was followed by a fielder's choice, a walk, and then two very solid singles, one to left and one to center, for a 2–4 day with a walk and run scored. With ten players in the field, it was tough to find an empty spot for a base hit, so when you bagged a couple, it felt that much better.

On the other hand, I can't tell you how proud I am of Barry. He wanted to foul tip a ball just once this week, and his experience would have been complete. I told him he would have at least five base hits, and he told me I was nuts. The first time up for the rookie was with the bases loaded and one out in the second inning. He broke his maiden with a ground ball single that the third baseman knocked down but couldn't play. Throw an RBI into the package as well. Two mediocre at-bats followed before his second hit of the game, a nice poke to left to keep the ninth-inning rally going. His line was 2–4, an RBI, a solid day in the field, and a huge "attaboy" for BarryO!

After the rough morning, the afternoon game was even tougher. The morning of nine innings combined with a long lunch break and a beating afternoon sun allowed the weariness to set in on all fronts. We played this game back at the Steinbrenner complex, though not in the stadium; instead, we were at an adjoining field with the stadium shining brightly in the background.

The Pinstripes fell behind by three runs in the first inning to a team coached by Mike Torrez and Orlando "El Duque" Hernandez. We tried to claw back, but lost 6–4 to go 0–2 on opening day.

Both of us had a forgettable afternoon. I just couldn't get comfortable at the plate and blamed JP's coaching as I promised him I would. I was 0–3 with a walk and an RBI. Barry was also hitless in three trips.

The best part about playing first base during camp (other than it's a short walk to the first base dugout) is that at some point during the day, Jake Gibbs, Al Downing, and Mike Torrez all coached first, and I enjoyed their company. I had a busy but mediocre day in the field with multiple chances and one miscue on a ball that was charged as an error to our shortstop but was one that I could have and should have knocked down.

Ironically, Downing and Torrez are members of a not-so-elite baseball pitching fraternity remembered for notorious pitches. Downing gave up Hank Aaron's record-breaking 715th home run while a Dodger in 1974. Four years later, Torrez, who left the Yankees after winning two World Series games in 1977, signed as a free agent in Boston and gave up Dent's memorable playoff round tripper. Torrez says time has moved him away from the spotlight and other than "a couple of guys that still gig me about it, nobody really remembers my role."

Of course for me, the most notorious pitch in baseball history was thrown by Ralph Terry of the Yankees to Bill Mazeroski on October 13, 1960.

Barry did fine in the field today. He split his time between second base and right field with ample defensive chances. Barry's big league experience continued this afternoon as the Yankee-owned YES Network did a dugout interview with him on his camp experience. He handled it like a pro and will be featured on Yankees Magazine television a few days after camp ends.

We both feel the strain of eighteen innings and are looking at another pair of nine-inning games tomorrow, but my day fell into perspective fairly easily. In seventeen years wearing a Yankees uniform, Mariano Rivera never had a base hit. In my first day in pinstripes, I have two!

Wednesday

Our team was made up of all Yankees camp rookies. I had a couple of camps under my belt as did one other guy on the team, but everyone else were breaking their maidens. Nearly all of the other seven teams were comprised of a good amount of camp vets who chose to play on the same team together. We seem to have gotten what was left. After our second doubleheader loss in a row on Wednesday afternoon, it was apparent that we were basically camp patchwork as we had now lost four straight. It looks like the laughs are going to have to happen off the field for me and Barry and that's the way today started.

While waiting for Barry, I spent a little hotel lobby time with former Yankees shortstop Bucky Dent. Bucky will always hold a soft spot in every Yankees fan's heart for the home run hit off Torrez in October 1978 to beat the hated Red Sox in a one-game playoff.

Bucky and I were chatting before heading to the Steinbrenner complex and Barry walked up. I introduced Bucky to my colleague. Barry stuck out his hand and in all earnestness said, "Hi, what's your name?"

What's your name? This is Bucky Dent. The Bucky Dent who arguably hit the most famous home run in Yankees history! The Bucky Dent who will forever be known as Bucky "F*c*i*g" Dent throughout New England! No true Yankees fan would ever have to ask Bucky Dent, "What's your name?" We know his name and will always cherish what he did for us on October 2, 1978. Bucky and I got a good laugh out of Barry's stumble and Barry, sheepishly, tried to explain to no avail his confusion by blaming it on the fact it was "early."

I couldn't let Barry off the hook. I later told Bucky that on the way to the stadium, Barry said to me, "Geez, the guy gets one hit in his life and I'm supposed to know who he is?" Bucky cracked up and responded, "Yeah, but it's on tape." Then he sat and had breakfast with us. Dent, a youthful looking sixty, said not one day goes by that someone doesn't bring up the home run. Fortunately, it's not the same for Mike Torrez.

We finished breakfast and walked by the training room. This line of beat up campers stretched out the door on only the second day. Not a good omen at all for the rest of the week.

The first kangaroo court of camp was on the docket before the morning games and was presided over by the very un-honorable Mickey Rivers.

Mickey played fifteen big league seasons, four with the Yankees in center field, and finished third in the 1976 MVP voting. He was known for his blazing speed, thus the moniker "Mick the Quick." He also was infamous for malapropisms, trailing only Yogi Berra on top of the Yankees list. When asked once by a reporter what his career goal was, Rivers answered, "To hit .300 and remain injury prone."

Unlike Pirates and Tigers camp, Rivers merely presided while the respective coaches did all the kangaroo court work. Court was held in the main gathering area of the clubhouse. Rivers was the judge, Bush the bailiff, and Gamble served as the clubhouse lawyer should anyone desire cheap and incompetent representation. Former Yankees pitcher Jeff Nelson turned his team in and fined them each $10 for applauding the opponents on Tuesday. As Nellie said, "The Yankees don't clap for the stinkin' Red Sox, and my guys are not going to clap for our opponents."

Then Barry got his camp court indoctrination. Rivers fined him $50 for not knowing who Bucky Dent was and told him an appeal was unacceptable. Before Barry could get out his wallet, our coach Homer Bush recommended another $10 fine for Barry getting doubled up on an infield fly rule on Tuesday to end our first game.

Almost on cue Dent yelled, "He had no idea who I was, how the hell would he know what the infield fly rule is?" The clubhouse broke up in laughter and Barry was leading the laugh brigade! It reminded me what a delight this guy is, and how lucky I am to have our friendship rekindled after all these years.

Unfortunately, it was then time to take the field. Our first game was against a team coached by perhaps two of the classiest guys to ever wear pinstripes, Roy White and Chris Chambliss. We fell behind early 9–3, rallied to tie it at nine in the seventh, and then unraveled like a cheap suit to lose 15–9.

Selfishly, it was a good game for me. I thoroughly enjoyed chatting with first base coach Chambliss, a resident of Atlanta, and the hitting coach for the Seattle Mariners. In what was a good personal defensive game, it's pretty neat to be told by one of the best who ever played my position, "Good hands and nice pick!" Positive reinforcement feels good at any age, but when Chris Chambliss says it to you while you're playing the position at which he excelled, it just feels that much better.

I had a good day at the plate with three solid shots to right-center in four at-bats. Barry had a single in four at-bats and an RBI. Physically, he's holding up incredibly well. As a bonus, he now knows who Bucky Dent is.

We were hurried through a quick lunch into the afternoon games as rain was forecast. On tap was a loaded, undefeated team coached by David Wells and Paul Blair, a team that hasn't lost a game in over two fantasy camps.

Wells was the marquee attraction among the ex-big leaguers this week. Boomer's reputation as eccentric preceded him, and early on you got the feeling he would be playing the prima donna card. During the opening night cocktail reception, the Yankees set up tables where the legends autographed all sorts of memorabilia for the campers, except for Wells, who didn't participate. Afterwards, an announcement was made that Wells would man a table by himself for autographs, one item per camper, following dinner.

Wells pitched in the bigs for twenty-one years with 239 regular season wins and another ten in the post season. He played for nine different teams, including a couple of two-year stints with the Yankees in 1997–98 and 2002–03. Wells gained notoriety for pitching an inning in 1997 wearing a 1932 Babe Ruth hat, his idol, and then in 1998 pitched a perfect game for the Yankees against Minnesota, admitting afterwards that he was hungover after being out the previous night at the *Saturday Night Live* cast party. He said what was on his mind, and was an easy guy to like if he pitched for your side but one to loathe if he was in enemy clothes. He retired following the 2007 season. These days he can be seen as a commentator on the TBS national broadcasts.

With all the hype, right down to the private autograph session, David Wells turned out to be just one of the guys—approachable, affable, and a leader in kangaroo court pranks. So much for first impressions.

We received encouraging pre-game words this afternoon from our coach Oscar Gamble before playing a game in which we were the decided underdogs. The Big O told us, "Let's take our drubbing and go home." That was much easier to comprehend than his legendary quote when he was still playing, "They don't think it be like it is but it do." Huh? He probably knew what was in store. The Wells-Blair team returned intact from last January's camp where they were a perfect 8–0. They entered this afternoon at 3–0, and their eleven-game winning streak was never in jeopardy.

We obliged and got drubbed. We actually had our first lead of the season with a 1–0 cushion in the second, but by the time the torrential downpour hit in the fourth inning, we were behind 9–3, and mercifully, the game was called.

I was 1–2 with a base hit to center. Barry only got up once and popped to first before the rain came. I felt a bit better about things on the field today and was pleased with a very challenging day on defense. Ground balls, line drives, stuff in the dirt—a real smorgasbord of opportunities with the glove. In a way, I like fielding more than hitting as I always felt challenged while playing defense as a kid, and now I know I can make the plays. I also spent an inning in the outfield, another first for me. I kept saying under my breath, "Please don't hit it to me, please don't hit it to me," and it worked. I was flawless on the right field grass. If I don't go back out there again, it might be too soon.

Four losses in four games—as many as I lost in the two previous camps combined, and we are only halfway through the schedule. Could be tough going the rest of the way.

Tomorrow will be interesting because for the first time, there will be inter-camp competition. Camp Yankees teams will play against the Detroit Tigers camp teams in a one-day tussle. I'm looking forward to seeing some of the guys we shared umbrellas with last year.

It's also family time for Barry and me. Andi came to Tampa last night. She has always encouraged me to go to camp and get out there and play, but she's never been able to see what the hubbub is all about. She clearly recognizes baseball talent when she sees it, and after watching our two games today she said, "You guys really suck." Thank you, dear.

Tonight Barry's wife Joan arrived with Barry's brother JerryO and sister-in-law Wendy. At least on Thursday we will have some friendly faces for what is shaping up to be our daily drubbing.

Thursday

The difference a day makes! This morning was simply the greatest baseball experience of my life.

The day started routinely enough when Barry and I headed to the Yankees complex for breakfast at seven fifteen a.m. As I do every morning, I asked the now-ironman how he was feeling and Barry said his groin was bothering him. I asked if it had anything to do with Joan coming to Tampa the night before. He said no. I called bullshit.

We got to the stadium with two games scheduled. We expected to take our morning spanking from a Yankees team that beat us once already and hoped we could muster enough gusto to beat the Detroit Tigers team we were slated to play in the afternoon.

The morning game was scheduled on Steinbrenner Field, spring home of the real Yankees, which was an unbelievable thrill. The Stadium is gorgeous, with seating for 11,000. Today we got the full scoreboard in operation and the Yankees brought to camp their Yankee Stadium PA announcer, Paul Olden, who introduced each batter and provided a running commentary of the game. It was incredible to not only be on the big field, but actually competing.

We faced the Torrez-El Duque team again. They beat us 9–6 on Tuesday afternoon and came into the game undefeated in four games; we came in winless in as many. At game time Barry's wife, brother, sister-in-law, Andi, and about fifteen other stragglers were on hand. They turned out to be our lucky charms.

Suddenly the gang that couldn't shoot straight erupted for eleven runs on twenty-two hits for a very comfortable and convincing 11–2 maiden-breaking win. Barry got his groin back in gear and was a smilin' 2–3 at the plate with a solid single to left-center in the first, which got Joan's attention. He even took his gimpy leg around the bases and scored a run.

I had the best day I've ever had on a ball field and accomplished my goal for the week with one swing of the stick. I was 3–4 with an RBI. Gamble and Bush have used me as the sixth hitter in the lineup for the last two days. That seemed to be my batting order spot across the board with the Pirates and Tigers, too. Quasi-flattering for an old guy. I hit into a force out the first time up and singled to the left side my second time. We exploded for eight runs in the sixth inning, and I got up with two down and a runner on first.

I drove the third pitch of the at-bat over the right fielder's head, and I knew I had to keep running. An extra base hit was my goal, and as the ball rolled into the 314-foot right field corner, I didn't even look for a cab. I just kept going. I got to second and that was it, goal achieved. My first one in three camps—my extra base hit!

It was a sweet feeling and a bonus to have Andi on hand. I returned to the dugout after my double, and Barry was waiting for me with a hug. He couldn't stop laughing. "What's so funny?" I asked. He said, "I haven't seen a Jew your age run that fast since I was at a Chinese buffet and they brought out the hot egg rolls."

That actually pushed the lead to 11–1, and the other guys were out of arms, so El Duque, allegedly forty-five years old but nobody seems to know the Cuban's age for certain, pitched the last three innings against us. Hernandez, a ninety-game winner in the big leagues with the Yankees, Mets, Diamondbacks, and White Sox, has 1,086 career strikeouts and a 4.13 ERA. He had an amazing 9–3 post-season record and earned four World Series championship rings, three with the Yankees in '98, '99, '00, and one with the White Sox in 2005.

I saw one pitch against him in my first at-bat and was drilled by a seventy mph fastball in the right calf. Ouch! Ten hours later, it still hurt. My second time up, I got the bat on the ball and hit a nubber down third base that the third baseman couldn't rumble over to get. I made it to first safely. It will look much better in the box score tomorrow: one for one and HBP against El Duque.

Barry's one at-bat against El Duque was hysterical. Bases were loaded, two out in the top of the ninth. Barry somehow worked the count full. On the next pitch, El Duque just reared back and ninety mph later, neither Barry nor anyone else knew what happened. Talk about heat. Barry stood there and took his punishment. El Duque, after getting the called third strike, ran off the mound and gave Barry a big hug. In his broken English, he apologized and said, "I had to do it, the bases were loaded."

My fantasy day was topped off by another real good game in the field that had me challenged and my uniform very dirty. The game ended with a shot down the first base line that I stopped like a hockey goalie on my knees and crawled to the bag before the runner got there.

A win on Steinbrenner Field in a major league setting, faced El Duque twice, got the long-awaited extra base hit, and my wife there to see it all. It doesn't get much better than this morning!

After lunch was the inter-camp series against the Detroit Tigers from Lakeland about forty minutes away. It was fun to see some of my cronies from last year and a teammate in particular that I was very fond of.

Our game was against one of the three visiting Detroit teams and clearly we like Thursdays since we coasted to an easy 4–1 win. We couldn't win a game on Tuesday or Wednesday but won 'em both on Thursday.

Pitching for the Tigers against us was former big leaguer Dan Petry, who won 125 games in his career. Dan threw nothing but junk at us, mainly knuckleballs, and coming from El Duque at seventy mph to Petry at forty mph was quite the contrast. Barry was 1–2 off the junk, and I was 1–3 and also got hit by a pitch again, but this time off my shoe. You don't really feel a knuckleball.

It was a good day for the Yankees campers all around as we won nine of the eleven games played today against Detroit. Why can't the real Yankees ever do as well against the Tigers in the playoffs? The Tiger campers by and large were big Midwestern boys, corn-fed and content. As Bucky Dent said, "I'm really proud of my guys. Not only did we sweep two games from the Tigers, but they outweighed us by about 2,000 pounds."

The differences between Yankees fantasy camp and the Tigers were apparent as the teams prepared for play in Tampa and Lakeland. The Yankees had two motor coaches pull up to Steinbrenner Field to take their traveling squads to Tigertown. The Detroit campers grumbled if they were assigned to play in Tampa because they had to round up as many private vehicles as they could find to make the trip.

Larry Rice came to Tampa as part of the Tigers entourage. He was my teammate in Lakeland last year. During the lunch break, he asked if he and a couple of guys could take a look at the Yankees clubhouse. We obliged. Words couldn't capture their expression.

After the minor league standards of the Tigers' facility, the Yankees' was truly magnificent. They stood there in awe and then took the very impressive walk up the clubhouse tunnel onto Steinbrenner Field, which even after two outings still gave me chills.

Another thing the Tigers didn't have to endure while in the Yankees clubhouse was a police state regarding shoes. The Yankees attendants couldn't have been more welcoming to our guests from Lakeland. It made me even more proud to be a Yankee.

So the gang that couldn't win a game all week won two games today. We have two more nine-inning games left tomorrow, including the first one back on Steinbrenner Field to wrap up the camp competition.

This is supposed to be our baseball fantasy, and this morning it truly was for me. It was a bonus getting to do it wearing pinstripes for the Pinstripes. It was the best game I have ever played from 1962 until today. I didn't see this day coming.

Friday

Evidently, the key to a winning streak after sweeping a doubleheader the day before is to know when to say when. Unfortunately, our guys didn't know how.

A very late night at the hotel lounge to savor the two-game sweep, after losing four in a row, led to cobwebs in the morning and a related thrashing. Unlike David Wells, we did not improve when playing with a hangover. Today was the last day of competition before the Legends game on Saturday. The Yankees don't use a playoff formula at camp. Eight games and whoever is left standing on Friday afternoon are the champs.

Kangaroo court saw hundreds of dollars raised for charity this morning, as things got a bit out of hand at the hotel bar on Thursday night. Campers saw fit to tell their Yankees coaches what they really thought of their strategy this week. The Yankees' charities now thank them all.

Somehow, I came out revenue positive in court as we weren't fined. However, I did win one of the raffle items this morning, a Wade Boggs-autographed baseball. I'm not exactly sure what I'll do with it and only hope he signed it as a Yankee and not a Red Sox, but the signature of the Hall of Famer will have some value on the open market one day.

A couple of baseball hijinks of note happened before we hit the field.

One of my Pinstripes teammates—for national security reasons let's call him Paul Appel—in his early forties and an FBI agent from Tampa, put on his baseball undergarment this morning only to learn that someone had sprayed IcyHot on the inside. If you want a real visual, for some reason our agent chose to wear Batman underwear. He jumped around looking for the perpetrator and walked through the whole clubhouse in his Batman underwear to get to the training room to seek whatever kind of specialty relief was available. He was laughingly angry and only wanted to know who did it. Wouldn't you think an FBI guy could solve a case like this? Solve the case of the salve.

The Travel Channel is here filming a piece about "The Ten Greatest Fantasies." As they interviewed a camper in the dugout, he got hit with a whipped cream pie from behind in typical Yankees celebratory fashion. It was all over the guy, but a Yankee tradition for the hero of a win.

Our first game this morning was against the team coached by Rivers and Dent. Barry now knows who Bucky is, and Dent reminds him every chance he gets. We were back on center stage, Steinbrenner Field, in front of a throng of approximately twenty close relatives. Retrieving a foul ball wasn't particularly difficult. Andi left for home this morning, but Barry's entourage remained.

The Rivers-Dent team was 3–3 with all their wins coming in morning games and all the losses coming in the afternoon. Their morning streak continued.

We took a pounding, still groggy from the celebration the night before, and lost 20–10 in a game stopped after eight innings because we were out of timeouts. Dent lobbied hard to stop the rout after six innings, but we insisted that we paid our money and wanted to play ball. Bucky was none too pleased and two innings later we finally conceded he was right.

There were fifty-three hits in the contest, twenty-eight by the other guys, and at times it resembled an adult version of a Little League game. For the first time all week, a trainer had to come out and stop play when an infielder decided to forego catching a pop-up with his glove and instead used his nose. By the time the game was mercifully stopped, Yankees PA announcer Olden was hoarse.

It still felt special to play in the gorgeous stadium and must have been to my liking as I had a 2–4 day with two RBIs and a run scored. That comes off a three-hit day in the stadium on Thursday. Both hits today were solid shots to the outfield, and now that the pressure is off with an extra base knock, I can refine my singles-hitting ability.

Barry, man of steel, awoke with minor groin problems again. He played the whole game in the outfield and was 0 for 3, but reached on a rare catcher's interference and wound up scoring a run.

Weariness set in throughout the entire camp, and most guys would need extra time boarding their flights on Sunday. Once again, the training room overflowed and those who bypassed therapy and went to lunch found the camp dietician to either be in a foul mood or a Red Sox fan. A scrumptious buffet awaited us featuring hamburgers, hot dogs, macaroni and cheese, sauerkraut, baked beans, onions, and fries—all those easily-digested entrées to take the edge off the ninety-degree heat index on the field.

We lumbered out for the afternoon game against the Jeff Nelson-Tanyon Sturtze team, both former Yankees pitchers and really good guys. Sturtze was the other uniform #56 in camp. They, too, have had a rough camp and entered the finale with the identical 2–5 record we sported. We hoped they didn't have a lighter option of salad and fruit for lunch.

It was billed as the "Battle for the Basement," or as one of our guys put it in his pre-game plea to us, "Let's show them we suck less than they do." Our boys must have been charged by that mantra because we got six runs in the first two innings and cruised to a 12–7 win and a final camp record of three wins and five losses. Yes, we did suck less than they do, and we managed to finish out of the cellar. We were proud.

By the time the afternoon game ended, everyone had had enough. Nobody walked as naturally as they did on Monday, especially our still-hopping FBI agent.

Actually, things on the field went a lot better for us the last two days, with three wins in four games. We just gave the first four away; otherwise, we were formidable. I'm not sure anyone saw three wins coming after a 0–4 start.

I ended well with a 2–4 game and a run scored. I saw and hit the ball very well today. Sunlight does that for an old guy. Barry kept smiling and my pride in him grew. Two solid singles to left, among his three or four best strokes of camp, gave him a 2–4 day as well, and he scored two runs. It was great to see him get around the bases and enjoy it so much.

Tonight the team took our coaches Gamble and Bush out for dinner. We had reservations at a nearby steak house. It turns out we shared a private room with the Torrez-El Duque team with whom we split our two games. During the evening, Torrez told us what he liked most about the week is "seeing guys with limited ability break their ass to live that major-league dream. I love it."

Our team, as seems to happen while spending a week together, developed a bond. The average age for our bunch, fifty-one, was by far the youngest team in a camp I've been a part of. The youngest on our team was thirty-nine years old, there were a couple in their forties, and our oldest was sixty-four. We came from five states: Florida, Alabama, California, Louisiana, and Georgia. Ironically, not one New Yawker was in our midst.

Discovering the mix of occupations among the guys is always fun. The Pinstripes consisted of a collegiate program director, an Oxford graduate who is a college professor/business consultant, a motorcycle shop owner, a cell phone tech pro, an owner of a chain of gas stations, a medical device sales rep, a guy in Internet marketing, a corporate exec at Subway, and a retired banker. Plus, we had two FBI agents from the local Tampa office, one with Batman underwear, and his colleague who probably will face a grand jury hearing for the IcyHot.

We were just twelve guys living our fantasy for a week brought together by age, a love for baseball, and in this case the Yankees. Fun week, fun group. We got there on Monday as strangers from all walks of life and left six days later with a special pinstripe bond.

Saturday

Mornings probably get better than this. I'm just not certain how.

Saturday was the final day of 2012 Yankees winter fantasy camp, and with the league play now concluded, all that remained was the Legends game, when the campers get to take on the guys who once upon a time wore the pinstripes for real and got paid instead of having to write a check for the experience.

Order of play was drawn by lot and our red-hot three wins in four games team drew the fifth of eight games on the day. The rules are pretty simple: a two-inning game where the campers get six outs per inning and the real Yankees get three. With twelve guys on a side, we all get to hit at least once.

And one other rule: the Yankees hate to get scored on.

Barry and I arrived at Steinbrenner Field during the first game of the day, and instead of going into the clubhouse to change to our blue uniforms, we went through the dugout runway to take in the sights.

On the sun-drenched field in glorious white pinstripes were Downing, Dent, Wells, Tiant, Rivers, Sturtze, Torrez, Gamble, Blomberg, Bush, Gibbs, Nelson, White, Blair, and Hernandez. Someone throw cold water on me, please, and wake me out of this Yankees dream! Like everything else this week, the Yankees camp staff did this day right, too. As each team took their turn on the diamond, the games started with pre-game camper introductions by Olden and the trot out to the third base line formation. When each camper came to bat, Olden gave a brief bio including their favorite Yankee, favorite Yankees moment, and favorite camp moment. The bonus was the picture of each camper on the scoreboard as he was introduced.

David Wells started for the Yankees against us and set the first six campers down with the help of two double plays. I was in the seventh spot of the batting order. When we came back around to hit, Wells was replaced. I can't believe I'm saying this, but I was a bit disappointed when Hernandez came in to pitch. I batted against him on Thursday and really wanted a taste of Wells, Jeff Nelson, or Tanyon Sturtze. After all, I owned El Duque. This ninety-game winner, four-time World Series champion struggled with me on Thursday, hit me in the leg the first time up, and then I "legged out" an infield hit. I wanted a different challenge.

It's pretty mind-blowing to step into the batter's box with your image on the center field scoreboard, El Duque on the hill, and Homer Bush and Bucky Dent up the middle. I never envisioned anything like this. I was reminded of the passion the boys in white have when the first pitch Duque threw to me was about eighty mph and right down the middle. The second was about the same but outside. The third was right down the pipe and I swung and missed. I asked him to slow it down a bit. He obliged with a forty-five mph sweeping curve ball. If it had been anywhere near the strike zone I would have looked awfully foolish. I had a two-ball, two-strike count, and a fastball down the middle I actually hit right on the button to shortstop Homer Bush, who tossed to first baseman Mickey Rivers to get me by about fifteen steps. I guess I no longer have El Duque's number.

Barry never had El Duque's number and unfortunately drew him again today. Fresh in Barry's mind was the blazing fastball strikeout on Thursday with the bases loaded. Today was more of the same, as three pitches later El Duque was done with Barry. Yankees staff estimated the strikeout pitch this morning was eighty-eight mph, a speed no sixty-one-year-old retired banker will ever catch up to and most major leaguers never did, either.

Defense was fun for me all week, and other than Thursday's double, it might have been the highlight of my camp stay. It was an eye-opening experience to be at first base and see three lefties—Rivers, Roy White, and Oscar Gamble—come at me in order. As a bonus, we actually doubled up Rivers on a 6–3 double play that our shortstop threw in the dirt, and when I looked down, the ball was in my glove.

We lost 1–0, the only team to hold them scoreless in their first at-bat. Bush beat us with a double to left in the second. More class was displayed as we walked through the post-game handshake line with the Yankees. Jeff Nelson thanked each of us personally for being here this week.

The closing banquet was well done. Each team was introduced, and the respective coaches had about five minutes to dish on their team. Then came the individual awards for the camp All-Star Team, Rookie of Camp, Most Valuable Player, and special honors. Two of our guys, Eli Gross and Richard Sosa, both in their early forties, were deservedly recognized on the All Camp team, something only the Yankees do.

As the curtain fell on the week, I kept going back and forth between how lucky I am to be able to do something like this and how wonderful the week truly was. The Yankees staff was terrific under the direction of Julie Kremer and AmySue Manzione. No detail was overlooked. This wasn't their first dance, and it showed. As I learned from my previous camp experiences, it's the small things that can make a huge difference. When we returned to our lockers after every game there was some kind of swag waiting for us: T-shirts, jackets, sweat shirts, golf shirts, sport shirts, sneakers, sandals, wine glasses, tote bags, and autographed balls by each legend. It never stopped and it all was top-of-the-line stuff. My son Jason said, "You pay $5,000 and they give you $350 in merchandise and you think you're getting a deal." True, in reality, we did pay for everything we received, but it was exciting to see what waited for us each day. The only thing they missed was a suitcase in which to bring it all home. Barry said, "I will never have to buy any Yankees stuff again. I have everything I need."

From the social events to the organized meals, the transportation to venues, playing on Steinbrenner Field, the professional clubhouse staff who made sure your laundry was done and ready for your next game and available for any other need, the training staff, and the photographers, everything was handled with effortless professionalism. I felt like both a welcomed guest and more importantly, a real ballplayer.

Best of all is that I feel much better physically than I have license to. A couple of aching quads but that's about it. I got beat up in the field this week, so I am thankful that's all that's ailing. I am proud of the defense I played. I answered the bell and first base at fantasy camp is a tough spot with infield throws that came from all directions in all shapes and sizes.

With staff pitching, we saw more hittable pitches than the norm and my numbers reflected as much. Initially I thought I wouldn't like six innings of staff pitching, but it actually turned out okay as it was serious, the games moved quickly, and the scores tended to be closer. I had a very good week with fourteen hits in twenty-eight at-bats, four RBIs, a walk, three runs scored, and got plunked twice by two ex-major leaguers, El Duque and Dan Petry. My batting average was .500. No complaints for a guy my age. I didn't strike out once, I put everything in play, and fourteen of them found holes. I realized I was 14–28 for the

Pittsburgh and Detroit camps combined, so the guy who wanted just to get one base hit two years ago can now post a 28–56 batting mark and not take a back seat to any other fifty-nine-year-old playing fantasy camp baseball and wearing #56.

Of course, the on-field goal for the week was reached on Thursday morning with my extra base hit, a double to the right field wall on Steinbrenner Field. All I wanted was one of those and I got it.

As great as the Yankees experience was, hanging out with old chum Barry for the week was the best part. Summer camp friends from 1965 to 1969 was followed by a thirty-eight-year hiatus which ended in 2007. He answered the call when I was looking for someone to be a Yankee with me for the week. It was as enjoyable as I thought it could be and more. In Yiddish, "mensch" is an expression to describe a person of strength and honor. Barry Otelsberg is a mensch.

He never played organized baseball in his life. Ten days before camp began, he was in bed with leg and back issues. A week before camp started, it was 50/50 that he would even make it.

He not only made it, but he was fun, fearless, and an all-star. His goal for the week was one foul ball. I told him the Vegas over/under line on total hits was 5.5. He told me I was nuts.

Barry's stats for the week were eight hits in twenty-four at-bats, five runs scored, two RBIs, and a .333 batting average. Way to go BarryO!

He rarely missed an inning. On his own, he moved from second base to the outfield to open up the spot for a more experienced player. He never asked for a pinch runner and was universally loved by all our teammates for the passion he brought to the game. I am so very proud and so very respectful of what he did. I'm glad I found Barry in my life again. His courage, dedication, commitment (and batting average) is something everyone can model themselves after.

It was a fabulous week, and I didn't think it could be better than the Pirates camp two years ago. But being a Yankees fan, surrounded by other real die-hard Yankees fans and all the past great stars, combined with the way this camp was operated, probably moved it to equal if not a notch above the Pirates experience, and the Pirates experience was a great one.

With the Yankees you sure get your money's worth of baseball for 5Gs. Eight nine-inning games or seventy-two innings of old-guy ball. Probably a little too much. The Pirates gave you about fifty-four innings or two full games less for a $1,200 difference. Maybe a little too little. What's more important—the innings or the cash? No idea how much baseball we were supposed to play with the Tigers because the weather never gave us a chance.

Having my wife on hand for a couple of days was very special as well. Andi got to experience part of the most wonderful week of the year. I asked her impression of what she saw. "A lot more real and serious than I thought it was going to be," she said.

We take growing old seriously. For one week, I can turn back the clock, or at least mentally, I can. I'm very grateful for what I've been given.

So what's next? I will be sixty this time next year. I'd love to play ball for a week with my two sons, Jason and Scott. This experience is right up their alley, and it would be a special treat and honor for me while I still have good health and some legs left to get through the seven days.

I can vividly remember throwing the ball with Dad on the side of our house in East Meadow. I remember tossing a ball with my kids when we lived in Wichita during their formative sports years and helping to coach their Little League teams. Now that my sons are grown men, I realize there is a potential opportunity for the bonus of a father-son fantasy camp experience. Many who attend camp are lucky enough to have their sons with them. Ray Kinsella never got that opportunity. I want do it while I still can.

The dream walk. From the Yankees clubhouse through the tunnel and out to shining George Steinbrenner Field.

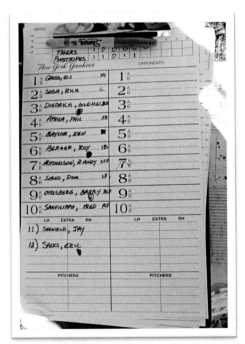

Never thought I'd see the day I was written into a Yankees lineup card.

Barry defends himself in court while Bucky Dent (over Barry's left shoulder) encourages a monetary sanction.

Talking first base strategy with Chris Chambliss.

Climbing the ladder after another off-target throw.

David Wells loosens up in the shadows of the NFL's Raymond James Stadium.

Homer Bush and Barry share a dugout laugh.

I am getting way too old to be playing in the dirt.

Doubling up the once-fleet Mickey Rivers.

Living the dream: making contact on El Duque with my image on the center field scoreboard at Steinbrenner Field. It's the epitome of the fantasy camp experience.

Sixth Inning

When Nature Calls

November 2012

I was on a high ten months ago as I packed up my baseball gear and left the Yankees clubhouse at Steinbrenner Field in Tampa. Yankees fantasy camp was actually better than I could imagine, and I longed for the day I could share the experience with my two sons.

I wanted to have my Ray Kinsella *Field of Dreams* cameo while I was still physically able to play ball. To spend a week in pinstripes with my lads under the Florida sun at the Yankees spring complex would be the ultimate fantasy camp experience. This was going to be the week, as the Yankees fall fantasy camp starts tomorrow.

However, it won't happen. Not this week, anyway.

Both boys are in California and neither can get away. Jason, thirty-one, is a TV writer and in prime writing season. Scott, twenty-nine, is an executive at a Beverly Hills luxury hotel and probably has used up his vacation days for the next twenty-five years following jam band Phish around the country.

Any hope of playing catch with them in a major league uniform has to wait, and at sixty, I'm just not sure how much more baseball time I have left. As someone wiser than I'll ever be once said, "If you want to make the Lord laugh, tell Him about your future plans."

With past camp-goers Pete being a one and done and BarryO on his way to India, the logical selection would be my oldest baseball-playing mate, my brother Mike. After a consult, Mike, fifty-seven, agreed but with the stipulation that if we were going to fantasy baseball camp together it had to be the Yankees. He's been a Yankees fan ever since I can remember, so he has license to pick the camp he wants to attend.

The first week of November seemed to be a schedule fit and tonight we planned to tuck into the Tampa Sheraton Suites, the Yankees fantasy camp home, for the next seven days. Awaiting us hacks as coaches were ex-Yankees from the January camp— Rivers, Dent, Bush, Downing, Gamble, White, Sturtze, Nelson, and Gibbs. They will be joined by Ron Guidry, Tony Kubek, Jessie Barfield, Gil Patterson, Fritz Peterson, Tommy John, and World Series perfect game legend Don Larsen. Truly from top to bottom as good a fantasy camp coaching lineup as you'll ever see.

We planned to arrive a day early to spend some time with Mom and Dad, who live over on the east coast of Florida in a retirement burg called Coconut Creek, or in Seinfeldian speech, "Del Boca Vista, Phase IV." We know we are lucky to still have Mom and Dad in our lives. Mom is eighty-two; Dad is eighty-three and he is still very active in the community. For the past sixty-three years, they have been known to all as Arlene and Herb.

We felt a quick visit before heading over to Tampa was in order, especially since Dad was such a strong baseball influence on Mike and me, and helped coach every team from the time we were the smallest of tykes.

One of my longstanding baseball recollections (circa 1962-ish) is with Mike throwing the baseball on the side of our house. We played a very scientific and advanced game we called pitcher-catcher. The rules were complex. One of us would pitch and the other would catch. A rulebook was not needed.

We also had to be pretty accurate since that side of our house was interrupted by the wooden retaining fence of our neighbors. Behind the fence and its overlapping trees lived two Doberman Pinschers. These weren't just ordinary Dobermans; Bally and Thane were baseball-eating Dobermans. They swallowed them whole, just for a snack. If a ball went over the fence, it was wise to just grab a new one from the garage. We had no interest in finding out if they also had an appetite for baseball players.

Back in the day, Mike was a much better ballplayer than me. He went on to a stellar Little League career that ended with one decision. Somewhere back around 1967 when Mike was twelve, he threw fireballs and was selected as the starting pitcher for the Central Nassau Little League All-Star game. The only caveat was he had to cut his hair before the game by league rule. His look was Tim Lincecum about twenty years before Tim Lincecum was born. Now Lincecum makes millions with Mike's hairstyle. In 1967, they could still dictate how you were supposed to look. That didn't last much longer.

According to lore, Mike refused to get a haircut and the game was played with someone else on the mound. That's all I can remember of his baseball career because soon afterward he swapped the glove for music, girls, long hair, and who-knows-what-else. Today, we would both pay big bucks to have that hair back.

I continued playing baseball into high school but Mike didn't. We reunited on the softball fields of South Florida for a while in the late seventies and early eighties, but it's been well over thirty-five years since we tossed a ball at each other and not had to worry about Bally and Thane. We planned to pick it back up tomorrow morning. There is a third Berger brother, fifty-two-year-old Ken, who still lives in East Meadow. Ken is a devout Mets fan who would spit on a Yankees uniform before wearing one, much like Mike and I feel about the Red Sox. Asking him to join us was never a consideration.

Mike calls Randolph, New Jersey, home and is very successful as a territory manager for food service giant US Foods. He is the consummate sales pro and calls some of New York City's finest restaurants, hotels, and clubs his account. He has been recognized many times at the top of the US Foods sales chain. He is lucky enough to have a great family, too. His wife Sue fought a long and fortunately victorious battle with ovarian cancer two years ago. Mike and Sue have twins, Kim and Brian. Kim is a recent graduate of The U where both Mike and I got our degrees. In fairness to Kim, the University of Miami she attended is much different than The U that Mike and I went to back in the seventies. We couldn't get admitted today. Kim is ticketed for med school. Brian, Kim's twin brother, gave up his first two years at Rutgers when he received acceptance at the US Military Academy at West

Point, New York. Brian is now completing his second year at West Point and will defend our country so guys like Mike and me can play baseball for a week. It makes an uncle beam with pride.

Though Mike's baseball career ended short of the barber's chair, he lived vicariously through their third child and youngest son Robby. Robby was the closer for the Randolph High School baseball team when they won the New Jersey State High School Championship in 2010 with Robby on the mound for the final out. It was a big thrill for all of us but especially for Mike, who was much more nervous than Robby during his games. Robby played collegiate baseball last year for Fairleigh Dickinson University in Madison, New Jersey, and Mike was along for every pitch.

Now, the reality of having to play baseball is hitting Mike. At his age, with his best days long behind him, the task seems a bit daunting. Being a three-camp veteran, I tried to prompt him on what he needs to do to properly prepare, but much like Pete from Tigers camp, I'm not sure that my suggestions registered. Mike does have a built-in advantage with Robby at home to mentor him.

This note arrived from Mike about a week ago: "*Not doing what I should to get ready. Went to batting cage last week and started in the sixty-five mph cage. Big mistake. Couldn't see the ball. After ten pitches, I switched to fifty mph. That was better. Threw with Robby for a couple of days and my arm still feels it. Didn't try to bend for a grounder. Need to take some ground balls, run the bases on a nearby field, and head back to the cage. I hope I can go the distance, though I'd be lying if I told you I wasn't worried.*"

I tried to caution Mike by reminding him that two years ago my Tigers teammate Pete Evans thought he was in great baseball shape and other than chew some bubble gum and watch a baseball game on ESPN Classic, he did nothing to prepare. His first at-bat, first step out of the batter's box, he pulled a hamstring and wasn't the same the rest of the week. By comparison, BarryO had a sciatic nerve compression a week before Yankees camp and couldn't get out of bed for three days. He was determined, struggled to get on the airplane, made it, and got through the week like a pro.

Compared to Pete and Barry, Mike has the potential to be all-world this week. With another workout or two and some good baseball luck, he shouldn't worry. He took the advice to heart.

A week later, I was talking to my sister-in-law Sue in advance of impending Superstorm Sandy to see how everyone was doing and how were they were preparing for the storm. She told me she and Robby were in the process of moving all the patio furniture inside and cleaning out the gutters.

"Where's Mike?" I asked. Sue said, "He went to the batting cage." Proud of that boy.

The next day, Sandy blew through and socked New Jersey. A tree in their front yard was dislodged and hit a power line, which blew a transformer to their house. They were scared when they smelled smoke. Six fire trucks and three police cars were at the house within thirty minutes, but fortunately, there was no fire. Like many who lived through Sandy, they were without power and there was transformer damage to the in-house utilities, but they were relatively lucky with death, devastation, debris, confusion, and panic only a few miles away. Sue and Mike, just like the rest of the country, saw the media coverage of what their

New York and New Jersey neighbors were living through with mouth-opening gasps.

On Tuesday, prior to our scheduled Saturday departure, Mike said, "Don't give this up yet. I still want to figure out a way to go to camp." On Wednesday, it looked doubtful. On Thursday, with litter and debris scattered everywhere, no traffic signals, some roads impassable, limited power back to their house, cold temps, no heat, and a two-and-a-half hour wait for gas (if you could even find a station open), Mike pulled the plug on our week.

"I just can't do it and I'm really upset," Mike said during the early morning phone call, "Will you still go?" he asked me. I told my brother if he didn't make the decision to cancel that I would have made it for him. You can't walk away from this and justify it. Though Sue was encouraging him, there was just no way. And no, I won't go without Mike. This was supposed to be our week together.

Julie Kremer, who very capably runs the Yankees fantasy camp, was understanding and sympathetic. She suggested accommodating us by rolling forward the non-refundable portion of the hefty tuition to a future camp date. We couldn't ask for more with only five days before the first pitch. We weren't the only ones she extended this courtesy to, though surprisingly, there were only about a dozen others who couldn't get away.

I asked Mike if he made the right decision. "Oh, yeah," he said, "there is no way I could have left all this mess behind." The good Lord willing, Mike and I will have our day again, hopefully during the same week next year. Maybe my sons can join us for what would be a fantastic experience for the four of us.

In the meantime, we think about all those in the path of Sandy who may not have their day in the sun for a long time. Unfortunately, having lived in both Kansas and Alabama for many years, I am all too familiar with the impact and residual damage of these natural disasters.

For eight years in Wichita, while I was the executive VP and general manager of Wichita Greyhound Park, tornadoes regularly occurred each spring and fall. We watched the radar and ducked for cover. The impact of the aftermath of those left in the wake, often times a matter of only a mile or two away from us, was an unforgettable sight. Just one week after we moved to Kansas in 1991, the infamous Andover Tornado swept through town and killed twenty-four people. The Weather Channel still uses video footage of the eye of that storm taken from underneath a Kansas Turnpike overpass. From our years in the Midwest we learned not to mess with Mother Nature, and if you have the luxury of time to prepare in advance, it's wise to get the heck out of her way.

Alabama has the daily double of tornados and hurricanes. Hurricane Katrina was a mind-numbing event. Even though Birmingham only experienced heavy rains and high winds, our city and her surrounding area became a refuge for thousands left homeless in the coastal areas of Alabama, Mississippi, and Louisiana. We were reminded of the impact daily for many months following. Most recently, on April 27, 2011, the F-5 tornado that just about wiped out Tuscaloosa, Alabama, also hit Birmingham. I was out of town that day, and Andi and Ibis spent a good portion of it sheltered under our house with heavy damage, loss of life, and wreckage less than a mile from home.

It's events like these and the residual from Superstorm Sandy that illustrate at times how insignificant throwing a baseball can be. Hopefully Mike and I will get another chance at the week together.

Right now, it's not appropriate.

Seventh Inning

Falling Apart

January 2013

Saturday

7 got "The Look" from him this morning. I know The Look. The objective of The Look is to lay guilt on me. The Look works 100 percent of the time. He's been with me virtually all his life and there's no mistaking it.

When the suitcase comes out, his bright, caramel eyes sink, and with an unmistakable sigh of disgust he lowers his cold, wet, black nose to the floor. This is very much unlike the look I get from my wife. Andi gets a twinkle in her eye and a little smile when the suitcase appears. She says not, but I know her "look," too.

Ibis is different. I know what this four-year-old, eighty-five-pound chow/retriever mix is thinking: *Do you have to leave again?* He's become my best friend, though admittedly the competition isn't that stiff. We serve each other's needs. I bombard him with treats, and he actually pays attention to me. It's a win-win.

This time The Look was a little different, because instead of the regular Samsonite travel carry-on suitcase, I've brought out a very large Adidas tote bag that's filled with stuff he doesn't see regularly—caps, baseball gloves, long- and short-sleeved undershirts, batting gloves, and a couple of baseball uniforms.

"That baseball thing again?" Ibis communicated. "You going back to that Yankees fantasy camp?"

Despite my wonderful experience in Tampa last January with about 100 other wannabes and never-weres, I told him, "Nope, heading to Bradenton, Florida, not very far from Tampa, for the Pittsburgh Pirates camp."

His ears popped up. "Pirates? Why the Pirates? They stink!"

I took exception to that. I turned and gazed at him. Ibis knew he hurt me. I started to tell him about the Washington Generals, who haven't won a basketball game since 1971, but I didn't think he'd really care. So I was nice.

"Well, old pal, it goes something like this…" I told him. "My first fantasy camp experience was three years ago in 2010 with the Pirates as they honored the 1960 World Championship team, my earliest baseball worship. You were too young to remember.

"I had a wonderful camp experience with the memory of the 1960 Bucs. Those long-ago idols have now become legends. At fifty-seven, I proved to myself I can still compete. It was followed by a throwaway camp in 2011 with the Detroit Tigers, as it was the only one that fit my schedule. Last year, I enjoyed a wonderful week with the Yankees and was joined by a dear childhood friend. If nothing else, I have three baseball cards and a dent in the bank account to show for the three camps, along with some great experiences and memories that at this stage in life, I never could have anticipated."

A chap from Pittsburgh I went to college with back in the seventies at The U dropped me a note after Yankees camp last February to ask where I was going next year. I told him I'd probably go back to the Yankees. "Why not Pittsburgh again?" he asked. Been there, done that. He asked what it would take to get me to go back. I told him the safest thing I could, that I'd go back in January if the Pirates have a winning season in 2012.

The Pirates haven't won more games than they lost since 1992, nineteen years ago. It's the longest streak without a winning season in professional sports history. In case you are ever faced with that Jeopardy! question, the next longest was the Philadelphia Phillies with sixteen straight losing years from 1933 to 1948, followed by the NBA Sacramento Kings and NHL Vancouver Canucks with fifteen. The NFL record for futility is Tampa Bay's fourteen years of losing.

The 2012 magic started to happen for the Pirates early in the season. Winning more than they were losing, the calendar reached August 8, and they were sixteen games over .500 with a record of 63–47 and only forty-two left to play. The Pirates sent out playoff ticket notices the same day I sent in my 2013 camp deposit. A promise is a promise.

Before my $750 check made it to camp coordinator Joe Billetdeaux at PNC Park in Pittsburgh, the threads started to show and the Pirates began to unravel. They proceeded to lose eighteen of the next twenty-three games, got no-hit by someone named Homer Bailey of Cincinnati on September 28, and then clinched it on September 30th by blowing a ninth-inning lead and losing to the Reds. It was their eighty-second loss of the season and twentieth straight year of failure. Incredibly, they finished 79–83, making it the greatest collapse in Major League Baseball history from where they stood the day my check went off in the mail. The Pirates truly were in an infamous class by themselves.

I e-mailed Billetdeaux. I could see the smile on Joe's face when he replied, "Read the small print. Deposits are non-refundable." Truth is, I planned to go to two camps this year anyway, had the Yankees in November with brother Mike not been scratched because of the northeast storm.

I had designs on this Pirate camp all along, as it played perfectly with my business schedule and the memory of how well things were run back in 2010, now that I have two other camps to compare. This was a must-return on my list. I also felt going back to Pirates camp would tie a neat little bow around this newfound yet expensive hobby of mine. My kids have grown and are established in their careers. Andi, though diagnosed with relapsing-remitting MS fifteen years ago, continues to live a very active tennis-laden lifestyle. My business, Medjet, has gotten stronger and more secure over the past three years. I relished the chance to go away for a worry-free week and not be a camp rookie anymore. Life all around is pretty good.

I was joined by ninety-five others at Pirate City in Bradenton who were equally anxious to put on a uniform to play out our major league careers that never materialized. The opening banquet was much different than it was for me my rookie year in 2010. Then, I showed up not knowing anyone else and walked into what felt like a class reunion for a school I didn't attend. I found out that 60–70 percent of campers are repeat customers and bonds are established. A 70 percent alumni rate and the fact this week could never get here soon enough has me convinced that camp truly is like a drug.

For some reason the Pirate campers of 2010, though not intentional, were very cliquey early on and didn't warm up immediately to the newcomers. Rather, the relationships built as we became teammates during the week, and by the end of the session six days later, everyone felt like old chums.

This camp is different for a couple of reasons. Even though it's my fourth fantasy camp, it's only my second with the Pirates, but at least I know what to expect. I've kept in touch with a couple of the guys from 2010 and many others were familiar faces, so the ice broke easily. In fact, as I walked into the reception tonight, I was greeted with a big case of déjà vu.

The first guy I saw was also a lonely rookie with me in 2010. Ron Lepionka, a corporate finance type from Atlanta, was celebrating his fiftieth birthday three years ago and now has returned for his fourth consecutive camp. Clearly addicted, he has evolved as one of the clubhouse leaders.

Also attending are two guys who were teammates of mine with the Tigers in 2011, Ward Brigham, forty-six, from Pearland, Texas, and Rico Ries, forty-four, from Tabor, New Jersey. Ward and Rico were fantasy camp nomads two years ago and ventured from camp to camp to find a place that fit. They'd been to the Reds, Braves, Yankees, and Tigers before I recommended the Pirates camp from my great experience the year before we were Detroit teammates. They came to Bradenton last year, loved it, won the camp championship, and are back again this year. Rico said, "I think we found a home." I was delighted to learn things worked out so well. The four of us had dinner together.

Billetdeaux is the camp coordinator. The director is former Pirates relief ace and submarine thrower Kent Tekulve, who is down for the count with a bug and may miss the entire week. The Pirates normally operate a Sunday to Sunday camp week. This year, they changed the scheduling to be Saturday to Saturday to allow the rabid Steelers fans time to get home in time to watch the Super Bowl next Sunday. The only thing missing will be the Steelers.

The 1960 World Championship team is represented again by four stalwarts with three being familiar faces from 2010—Bill Mazeroski, Vernon Law, and Bill Virdon. The fourth is Elroy Face, a personal favorite of mine, who was the Pirates relief pitcher extraordinaire that championship season. Maz, at seventy-six, is the junior member of the featured foursome.

Also on hand to have a cocktail and spin a tale or two are former Pirates from more contemporary generations, including Steve Blass, John Candelaria, Dave Cash, Richie Hebner, Grant Jackson, Mike LaValliere, Omar Moreno, Bob Robertson, Don Robinson, Manny Sanguillen, Zane Smith, and Bob Walk.

Before I left Birmingham, I tried to explain to Ibis that some guys like to go hunting or camping or fishing. I like playing baseball. Former New York Giants quarterback Phil Simms once said, "You play until you physically can't play anymore."

I'm lucky. At sixty, the clock is ticking but I can still play. I doubt Ibis understands.

Sunday

Experience is a great teacher. Especially if you learn a lesson.

Three years ago and on the first day of my newfound baseball fantasy, I walked into the morning breakfast in the Pirate City cafeteria and it looked like the tarmac at ATL's Hartsfield airport. Tote bags, duffel bags, bat cases, you name it, were all scattered in the front of the room while their owners stood in line for a plate of eggs and a biscuit.

Not me. Frankly, I had never given it a second thought until I was ready to leave my dorm room that morning and head downstairs. At that point, I realized I needed something to carry my glove, shoes, batting gloves, Aleve, Band-Aids and other assorted gels, creams, and PEDs. I grabbed the first thing I could find, which happened to be a Westin Hotel laundry bag.

The embarrassment I felt when I walked in carrying a laundry bag to breakfast when everyone else had a proper sports bag still lingers. It was a real rookie mistake that could have been glaring but fortunately nobody noticed.

I surely learned my lesson, so this morning I proudly ventured in with my New York Rangers tote bag. I'm not sure of its origins, but I brought it with me in 2011 to Tigers camp and have stayed injury free with a few base hits along the way. Ever since then, I've considered it a camp staple. Not that I'm superstitious or anything.

The one thing I left in the room this morning was my mate for the week. I just couldn't bring myself to bring her down to breakfast. I didn't want to be that guy who shows up at a pool hall carrying his own cue stick. It either screams, "I'm good," or, "I'm no good but want you to think I am." Since neither applies in my case, she stayed in the room during breakfast.

Mike Hallman has been a professional colleague and friend for the past twenty-five years. For the holidays last month, he gave me a personalized maple wood Louisville Slugger bat, complete with a Pirates logo and my own signature model. I've got to admit I thought it was pretty cool. I wasn't sure if he meant it for display or actual use, but I decided to use it. My wife said, "Mike gives the best gifts." I told her time would tell.

Two years ago, Mike gave me the first baseman's glove. I guess he felt a little sorry for me having to go through 2010 Pirates camp with my 1962 model which broke a string every time I caught a ball. The new one actually worked wonders for me. I'm hoping "TheBat" is half as good.

In past camps, I would choose my designated piece of lumber from the camp supply prior to the first game. I usually fell in love pretty quickly, and I would go out of my way in between my at-bats to selfishly stash my weapon somewhere that made it hard for the other guys to find. Too much risk in sharing a bat; there are only so many good hits in each stick, and I wanted them all for myself.

Promptly at 8:05 this morning, the processional from the cafeteria to the Pirates clubhouse began. If you didn't know better, you'd think they were assembling the ninety-six campers for a synchronized march down Broadway on Thanksgiving morning. We paraded to the clubhouse for the uniform unveiling.

The campers on the roster this year range in age from thirty to seventy-four with the average of fifty-four. Most come from the Pittsburgh metro area, 71 percent between Pennsylvania, West Virginia, and Ohio. A total of fifteen states are represented; three are from California, the furthest distance. There is only one from Alabama. Rookies make up 30 percent of the roster.

Pirate City is a beautiful complex and the nicest compound of the three camps I've attended. The Pirates have everything on one tract of land, including a dormitory that eliminates the need for a local hotel and the shuttle back and forth from the playing complex. The $20 million renovation in 2008 gives the main building the feel of a hotel with lounges, Ping-Pong and pool tables, and easy seating throughout.

When I made my way over to the familiar dorms, I shook my head when I got into my room. I thought I had heard of all the old-time Pirates greats. Not my room dedication, however; someone named Bob Elliott, who played for Pittsburgh from 1939 to 1946 and was a three-time all-star. He was traded to Boston in 1947 and then became the league's MVP. Figures. I called Dad. "Ever hear of Bob Elliott?" I asked. "Sure, he was a great third baseman for the Pirates who they wound up trading away," Dad said. That was good enough for me, so I unpacked. I'm past the roommate stage of life and had paid a few extra dollars for a single and smuggled TheBat in with me.

A short walk on either side of the dorm is the attached cafeteria/banquet hall where all meals and events take place during camp week. On the other side is the clubhouse/locker room. Outside of the clubhouse, about a nine iron away, are the four major league playing fields that will test our limits. There is also a twelve-mound bullpen area and six all-weather hitting cages to refine the swing we never had.

The main clubhouse is spectacular, major-league in every way with wooden finishes throughout and enough staff to satisfy your every whim. Truly, we have the big-league experience, which includes having our uniforms and undergarments washed nightly and our shoes shined before the next day's games. In fact, it's a policy I am thinking of instituting at home.

Everyone has their own personalized locker in which hang two uniforms—a home Pirates formal white and a bit more casual away black top, with pants, socks, belts, and hats—the whole baseball enchilada. After all, we are major leaguers for the week.

The rookies walked in and were wowed, while we vets knew what to expect but looked forward to the parade every time—try on your uniform, make sure everything fits, and then get ready to hit the field for the morning evaluation game.

Arguably, the loneliest number in baseball has to be #60. Back in my day, nobody notable in baseball wore #60, unless you were a twenty-eighth round draft choice, invited to major league camp, given #60 for a day or two, and then shipped out to baseball purgatory in Dubuque or Paducah or Oneonta. If you ever came back, you have proved your mettle and were then given a real number to wear. However things have changed over the last decade or so, and higher numbers have become trendy and even commonplace.

In the annals of sport there is only one #60 of any renown. For reasons unknown, NFL Hall of Famer and Cleveland Browns quarterback (yep, QB) Otto Graham wore #60 during his playing years in the late 1940s and 50s. In today's NFL, quarterbacks are forbidden by rule to wear a number that high; in fact, all position numbers are now mandated by rule in football.

But there they were on Sunday morning when we marched into the clubhouse—my two Pirates uniforms—a traditional home white with Pirates across the chest and the alternate black with a sharp "P" on the breast and "Berger" and "60" stitched onto the back. If I was doing this for a living and saw #60, I wouldn't unpack too quickly.

For the past three years, I had worn #56 with the Pirates, Tigers, and Yankees. All three uniforms are retired now and hang in the comfort of our guest room closet with no foreseeable avenue to ever be worn again.

I wore #56 the last three years because I didn't want to disgrace the memory of my past favorites, Roberto Clemente #21, and Thurman Munson #15, with my play on the field. This year I chose #60 to commemorate my age and in homage to the 1960 World Champion Pirates.

With everyone distracted by their newfound baseball goodies in the clubhouse, I was able to slip back to the dorm undetected to grab TheBat.

The evaluation game of five innings gives the brass a chance to separate position players so everyone gets fair playing time. In truth, with only twelve to a team, we will get all the time we want because the injury bug will hit in game one and grow during the week. The other camps didn't play an evaluation game, but instead, simply divvied up the teams prior to arrival. At least the Tigers asked for a position preference on their sign-up form. The Yankees did not play an evaluation game, and with no preference request, you run the risk of getting three of me on a team and all of us being unhappy. The Pirates do it the right way.

In this morning's evaluation game, we batted in alphabetical order and our randomly selected team hit first. With no As on the roster, I was the first batter in the first game of camp as it was three years ago, this time on a gorgeous Chamber of Commerce day. It was an immediate test for TheBat. With the count worked to 3–2, she saw the slowest pitch of her young life and laced it over the third baseman's head to break her maiden and got her very first hit in her very first try. Attagirl!

With her first test behind us, the rest of the game went just fine. We won 11–0, meaning nothing, and I finished the day 1–2 with a walk and an RBI. I had a good day in the field as well and was challenged from just about every angle from guys whose best throws were over twenty years ago.

After morning play, the coaches were sequestered to a secret hiding place and theoretically, the player draft began. More than likely it's closer to a World Wrestling Entertainment board meeting. With only about twenty-five rookies in camp, the brass knows who can do what and the best way to even out the teams. The campers had lunch in the cafeteria in the interim and waited for a proverbial sign of white smoke to indicate the decisions were made.

I'm realistic that I won't be invited to the green room as a first rounder. I figured between my advancing age and a quasi-track record of still being able to compete, I am probably somewhere in the middle, say a sixth or seventh round pick. (See Mom and Dad—I told you I would get drafted by the Pirates. It just took about forty years longer than planned.)

Finally, after about ninety minutes of everyone milling around the clubhouse bulletin board, the door to the coaches' room opened and the teams for the week were posted. Nobody has any idea how or why they were selected. Each team was named after a

Pirate legend of the past. "Bob Elliott" was not one of the team names.

The coaching pairs are decided in advance, and this 1960s Pirates fan would have loved to play for the combination of Vern Law and Bill Mazeroski or Roy Face and Bill Virdon. Mike LaValliere and Don Robinson would not have been my first choice. I doubt I was theirs, either. However, we are now hitched for the week.

LaValliere, known as "Spanky" during his playing days, was an outstanding defensive catcher for the Pirates from 1987 to 1993 with a lifetime .268 batting average. Spanky, now fifty-two years old, was a fireplug listed as 5'8", 190 pounds during his playing days but in reality was probably an inch or two shorter and maybe a dozen pounds heavier. He was one of the slowest runners in MLB history, which may be the reason I am paired with him.

Robinson, fifty-five, pitched for the Pirates from 1978 to '87 with 109 career wins. He was known as an outstanding hitting pitcher with thirteen big-league home runs, including a pinch hit HR in 1990, the first time in twenty years a pitcher hit a pinch hit dinger. He was part of the Pirates World Championship pitching staff in 1979 and goes down in baseball history as the hurler that gave up Mike Schmidt's 500th homer in 1987.

Our team, the Traynors, was named after Pirate great Pie Traynor, who played back in the Bob Elliott days. Our afternoon opener was against the Vaughans, managed by Vernon Law and former Pirates slugging first baseman Bob Robertson.

I was pleasantly surprised by LaValliere and Robinson. During their time with the Pirates, my allegiance had shifted to the

Yankees, so I didn't follow their careers; thus the initial indifference when I found out they would be my coaches. They were extremely personable and very engaged, though their once-ballplayer physiques have fallen victim to multiple buffets. They crossed paths only briefly as teammates on the Pirates in 1987 but remain close friends today. Both live in Bradenton and were partners for many years in a local baseball academy, without Ike Blessitt. The chemistry between them is evident.

Prior to the game, Spanky ran through our set of signs, including the steal sign for a game with no stealing. "If I have the steal on, I will jump in the air and not come back down," he told us. Nobody stole a base.

We piled on the Vaughans early and never looked back with a 17–6 win under a hot eighty-degree Bradenton sun. I was penciled in at first base and batting sixth, the spot in the order that seemed to suit my skill level at the previous camps. TheBat and I had a very good afternoon with a three for five game, including three RBIs and two runs scored. My last two at-bats were solid shots down the right field line that probably would have gone for a double for everyone but Spanky and me. I managed to stretch each of them into singles in what was a "TV" game for the camp DVD.

LaValliere and Robinson actively coached the entire game, moved guys into position, encouraged us, and kept things light. It was fun. Of the six coaches I've played for previously—Bill Virdon, Jerry Reuss, Frank Tanana, Darrell Evans, Oscar Gamble, and Homer Bush—Spanky and Robinson were easily the most engaged in our game, and frankly, it was nice to see.

We are probably a middle-of-the-pack team with a few guys who can pitch, and that's the key in fantasy camp, which at times resembles what adult Little League might be. The other guys couldn't pitch today and that was the eleven-run difference.

The toughest thing to watch was when one of our teammates, sixty-two-year-old Brent McCall, took an awful spill. McCall rounded second, headed to third, and went down with a thud. A partial tear of the Achilles had this rookie camper headed for surgery in the morning with not one full game under his belt. He was devastated and we all felt his pain. We are down to eleven players with little room for further injuries.

It was a nice start for me and TheBat. Our personal line score is four hits in seven at-bats, four RBIs, two runs scored, and a walk.

We have a doubleheader tomorrow. Shhhh. I'm tired. TheBat and I need some rest.

Monday

From coast to coast, there couldn't be a better day than today, and my pride stretched from Bradenton, Florida, to Hollywood, California.

We were greeted this Monday by another gorgeous sunny morning with two games on the schedule. After only one day of camp, most guys were walking like they just came off the set of *Bonanza*. Following the morning briefing and a painful group stretch, we took batting practice. The Pirates are the only camp I've been to that lets you take live batting practice on the field before the day's first game. The cage is up, and each team gets about twenty minutes to loosen up with the opposing team shagging.

When I got my cuts, I asked LaValliere to keep an eye on my swing. Spanky was a left-handed hitter, even though he was a catcher. Immediately, he caught a flaw in my follow-through, one of many I'm certain. The adjustment made an incredible difference in the ball flight. I was feeling really good about things until my second-to-last swing, when I lost my roommate. She shattered and I was shattered. TheBat took all the pounding she could and left me solo for the rest of the week. A nice crack right up the middle of the shaft spelled history for this fine gift, which I'm now thinking was more for show than dough. She met an unfitting sendoff as part of the day's trash from the field. It's a pity—we had such a good opening day together and were just getting comfortable with each other. I would have cried, but there's no crying in baseball.

As I stepped out of the cage, Richie Hebner, a seventeen-year major-league vet with the Pirates, Phillies, Mets, Tigers, and Cubs called me over. Through his very thick Boston brogue he asked, "Berger, do you play golf?"

"Yes, very poorly," I replied.

He asked me to show him my golf swing and then he said, "You need to pivot with the back foot when hitting a baseball just like you do on your golf swing." This guy won a World Championship with the Pirates in 1971 and also was a batting coach with Boston and Philadelphia, so I really couldn't slough off his suggestion.

In the bottom of the first, I walked up to the plate with one of the camp inventory bats that I scrambled to find after placing

TheBat in her final resting place. It's a brown Louisville Slugger and the color makes it easier to recognize among the dozen bats on the rack. It felt good and I didn't have time to test drive many others. There was a runner on second, two out, and the count two balls and a strike. I followed through with my swing, pivoted, and hit the ball further than I've ever hit one in my life. I knew it was going to be good as soon as it left what instantly became my new favorite stick. I saw the right fielder turn and start running. The ball bounced twice to the fence, 335 feet away, and I actually coasted into second with a double and an RBI. I probably could have made third, but I took one look and third base seemed too far away with the refrigerator I was carrying on my back. I reckoned a double was very nice, indeed.

As the inning ended and I ran back to the dugout, I looked at Hebner on the other side. "That's the last damn piece of fuckin' advice you're getting from me," he yelled with a smile.

The truth is, last year at Yankees camp on Steinbrenner Field, I hit a similar shot that went into the right field corner 314 feet away, also for a double, my first extra-base hit in any camp. Today's was even better. I hit the ball right on the dot and the only thing that stopped it from rolling was the 335 fence. Stuff this good at my age shouldn't be happening!

My second time up, the BrownBomber found the groove again, but with the right fielder backed up a few steps, it turned into a routine fly ball for an out. My third time at-bat really left my head spinning. With runners on first and second and nobody out, Bob Walk, a 105-game winner in the major leagues and Hebner's coaching partner, called time and came to the mound to actually rearrange the defense for me. Walk does the color commentary on the Pirates telecasts so he knows a thing or two about strategy. He shifted outfielders and repositioned infielders. I stood there in disbelief. Jerry Nelson, fifty-two years old from Hudson, Ohio, was pitching and was the hardest thrower I've faced yet in three games this week. With a fastball in the low sixties, he got me swinging late and I popped out to the shortstop. However, I was really, really flattered by Bob Walk's attention.

We went on to win the game in a 9–1 rout. That's the good news. The bad news is we lost two more guys. Dr. Jay Petruska, fifty, strained a hamstring, and Gary Dmitrzak, fifty-two and potentially our best player, was carted off the field with a heel injury. Gary had surgery on the same heel four months ago. His doctor told him to stay off it for six months, and these guys don't get their medical degrees by not knowing their trade. To make matters even worse, Dmitrzak and Brent McCall, our Achilles-tear guy from Sunday, are brothers-in-law. Not a good couple of days for this family.

We were down to nine able bodies including mine, which was scary. After a lunch break and my constant thoughts about how things were going 2,500 miles to the west, we took our 2–0 record and finished our division schedule against the only winless team in our division, coached by two of my 1960 heroes, Virdon and Face.

Mr. Virdon, eighty-one years young, was of course my coach in 2010. Face was the Pirates stopper in the bullpen for the 1960 World Champions following his 1959 season when he posted an 18–1 record as a reliever throwing his trademarked fork ball. An eighteen-win season for a relief pitcher will never happen again in this era of inning specialists. Face, only 5'8", 155 pounds in his prime, would come in as early as the sixth inning in a tied game, or maybe one the Pirates trailed, and they'd come back and he'd get the win. He was the "closer" a decade or two before we even knew there were "closers."

The game was different back then. Pitchers were not role players as today; they went as long as they could, as often as they could, especially out of the bullpen. Face is eighty-four years old, but you would never know it by looking at him. If I look closely, I can still see that thirty-year-old profile from his baseball card and hear Pirate announcer Bob Prince say, "And in from the bullpen comes little Elroy Face."

If there ever was a trap game, this was it. We were unbeaten, they were winless, and you know the rest of the story. Almost. We trailed 3–2 in the bottom of the sixth, and with some real aggressive base coaching by LaValliere and a key two-out, two-run single by Dean DeLuca (yes, Dean DeLuca, not Dean &...), this team, now held together by an ACE bandage, rallied to score three runs and take a 5–3 lead to the seventh.

I was 0–1 with two walks and really didn't contribute much until the top of the seventh. The game was played on the only Pirate City field with artificial turf, and the ball came off much faster and sharper than on dirt and grass. The Wagners put runners on first and second with nobody out in the final inning. Then a hard-hit ground ball to our third baseman Greg Gasparich, forty-five, resulted in a force at third and the long throw over to me. The ball skipped off the carpet and into my glove for a double play. The game ended in almost identical fashion one batter later, when shortstop Todd Rowley, forty-eight, fielded a grounder that I picked up out of the dirt to get the runner by half a step as we preserved the 5–3 victory.

My first handshake with hero Elroy Face was in the post-game "nice game" line. Who would have thunk it?

The day started with TheBat, replaced quickly by the BrownBomber, and ended with TheGlove.

We must be the most fragile 3–0 team in camp. It's also the second time in as many Pirates camps that I've been on a club that started 3–0. By sweeping our division, we have already qualified for Thursday's playoff round (if we have enough bodies left), and tomorrow will be nice for the nine of us remaining as we have only one game in the morning. We can use the afternoon in the whirlpool.

Despite the doubleheader sweep, hitting the longest blast I've ever hit in a baseball uniform, and a couple of defensive stops to help win a game, all day my mind was in Hollywood, California, at the production set of Paramount Studios.

Nothing makes a parent prouder than seeing a child reach their goal. Not even a 335-foot shot to the right field wall. My son Jason has longed to be a television comedy writer his entire life. He got knocked around for a few years after college as is the norm in that trade. But at 6:30 a.m. Pacific time today, production began on his first script, an episode of ABC's comedy *Happy Endings* that will air in the spring, the culmination of a dream.

Perhaps it's ironic, but maybe the perfect place for me today was on a baseball field. If I was home or in the office, my mind would have constantly been on the production set and wanting to know how things were going. If I weren't on the field, I would more than likely be in LA, a place Jason didn't need me to be today, nor would younger son Scott want me around to offer my help in running The Peninsula Hotel. My place is clearly in Bradenton, worrying about sixty mph fastballs and throws in the dirt as my boys do their thing, and baseball remains our common sports thread.

So a huge tip of the Pirates cap to Jason. No matter what happened today in Bradenton, you had a better day than me. I'm proud of you!

Tuesday

It's day three of Pittsburgh Pirates fantasy camp on a sunny, warm and windy Tuesday and I had the pleasure of having breakfast with one of the greatest Pirates of all time, pitcher Vernon Law.

The "Deacon," as he is known, has been ordained into the priesthood of the LDS Church and now lives in Provo, Utah. He was a stalwart of the 1960 World Championship Pirates with a 20–9 regular season record, was named to the National League All-Star team, and was bestowed the highest honor a pitcher can receive with the 1960 Cy Young Award. He also won two of the four World Series games the Pirates needed to beat the Yankees that fall. Good-naturedly he still claims if manager Danny Murtaugh had not removed him from Game 7 in the sixth inning, he would have closed the door on the Yankees and nobody would have ever heard of Bill Mazeroski.

Still sharp at eighty-two, the Deacon is very active in the Mormon Church. After retirement he coached baseball at BYU for ten years and finally called it a career in 1979. He was cordial and frank this morning. He said the late Stan Musial was his toughest out because "you knew he would put the ball in play somewhere." Law made $35,000 in 1960 and said a rookie that signs today for $480,000, the minimum, makes "more than I did in my whole career." A discussion ensued about the economics of today's ballplayers being a precious and expensive commodity to the team that signs them and the financial liability that results. In Law's day, the average major league salary was $6,000. Today, it's $3.4 million. The guys from the fifties and sixties recognize they paved the way for today's outrageous salaries yet don't seem bitter at all. So much has changed with the economics of sports, and they consider themselves pioneers.

Law has his hands full with six children (all first names starting with a V), including former major leaguer Vance Law, who have produced thirty-one grandchildren and thirty-two great grandchildren. We didn't have enough coffee left to see if he could name them all.

Today's schedule called for only a single game, and most of us were greatly relieved. We were supposed to play downtown at McKechnie Field where the Pirates play their spring games, but the stadium is under renovation, and unfortunately, the schedule shifted back to the fields at Pirate City. I was disappointed because I love the stadium setting and the big-league feel.

A surprise guest at our morning briefing was Pirates manager Clint Hurdle. A very engaging and funny man, Hurdle played ten years in the bigs before becoming manager of the Colorado Rockies and taking them to the 2007 World Series. In his third year with the Pirates, Hurdle still feels the sting of last year's collapse and the run of twenty straight losing seasons.

He gave the campers hope and enthusiasm by handicapping the team he has coming back and left little doubt the Pirates will contend right until the finish line. There's no question in Hurdle's mind the twenty-year losing streak ends in 2013. He said, "Not a day goes by that I don't think about a World Championship in Pittsburgh," as a huge cheer erupted from the camp. He also told us, "I know everyone here can do my job better than I can. I hear that every day, and I've found the best managers in baseball tend to be barbers and cab drivers." He then delivered some depressing news for the campers by announcing, "If you think by the way you play today I'm going to sign you, please forget about it."

The baseball camp staple of kangaroo court was first on the day's agenda. It's our chance to chuckle at the expense of dubious and embarrassing feats from the day before both on and off the field. Our coaches also serve as double agents; any foibles they feel worthy of mention are turned into the judge for "recognition" among the whole camp.

Presiding Judge Steve Blass, seventy, had an interesting big league career, all with Pittsburgh. As a right-handed fireballer, he won 103 games against seventy-six losses in a ten-year résumé with a lifetime 3.63 ERA. His best season was 1968 when Steve rang up eighteen wins and a 2.12 ERA. His highlight reel begins with the 1971 World Series, which the Pirates won in seven games over Baltimore. Blass had two complete game wins, giving up only seven hits and two runs. He was second in the Series MVP voting behind the great Roberto Clemente, then things went wrong for the Connecticut native. Very wrong. In 1973, Blass lost the strike zone, his ERA jumped to 9.85, and he was finished. He spent 1974 in the minors, and by 1975 he was a salesman for a company selling class rings.

His on-field achievements did not become his legacy; instead, his inability to find the target became baseball lexicon. Now, others who lose the ability to throw the ball accurately are labeled as having "Steve Blass Disease," among them Steve Sax, Rick Ankiel, Chuck Knoblauch, Mark Wohlers, and Dontrelle Willis. I'm pretty sure New York Jets quarterback Mark Sanchez has it too.

Blass may have lost the strike zone, but he didn't lose his hand-eye coordination on the golf course. In September 2009, Steve miraculously made not just one, but two holes-in-one during the same round, acing two par 3s, one at 154 yards and the second 175 yards away. What are the odds of making two holes-in-one in a single round? Just a cool sixty-seven million to one!

Blass hasn't lost his sense of humor, as was evident in his kangaroo court gig each morning. He is a one-man court posse for the Pirates.

The Pirates maintain a reasonable fine structure of $1, $2, or $5, depending on the transgression. Over the years, I've paid my fair share of fines for wearing the wrong attire (three times), standing in the wrong place during court, not settling down my pitcher when he got in trouble, talking back to the judge, giving poor base running instructions, and being on a team that sucked. If my fines were totaled, and considering everything goes to charity, I could probably move into a lower tax bracket.

Over the last couple of days, Blass fined one camper for catching a ball with his ear; one guy got slapped because his wife went up to his coach and suggested a better position for her husband to play; another caught for an entire inning without a chest protector; another for wearing shin guards under his uniform pants to stop a ground ball. One gent made eleven errors and Blass said, "Ironically enough, he works for the Department of Defense." Eight guys were fined for being in the cold tub together. Coach Bob Walk was fined for actually walking up to home plate as a member of the Phillies in 1980 to hit without a bat, and eighty-four-year-old Elroy Face was fined for "still driving a 1989 Lincoln and wanting people to think he's a pimp."

Blass generously offered a $1 credit to any camper wearing #28, his uniform number.

I thought I would save money this camp, but I got zonked as well. I was fined $1 for going to Detroit fantasy camp and $2 for going to Yankees camp last year. The mere mention of "Yankees camp" drew a hearty round of boos from the other campers. It's so much fun to be a Yankee.

Finally, it was game time for the single contest on the day's slate. I was surprised to find out our troupe of nine was the only undefeated team left in camp at 3–0; not bad for a group of guys held together by IcyHot and bandages. Our opponent today was the formidable team of Hall of Famer Bill Mazeroski and Blass. Blass has a reputation among the other coaches of wanting to win every year, and the team he drafted probably was the pre-camp favorite to win it all. Maz, on the other hand, prefers to sit and enjoy his cigar no matter the time of day.

We faced the best player on the grounds, Denis Dunlap from Irwin, Pennsylvania. Dunlap played Division I college baseball at East Carolina. Not only is he one of the youngest in camp at thirty-eight, he's also the most talented. He was the obvious Blass-Mazeroski choice to pitch this morning in a game they needed to win to qualify for Thursday's playoffs in a tougher and better-balanced division than the one we coasted through.

I got to hit against Dunlap in the first inning. Throwing in the mid to high sixties, the ball looks like a different object than you regularly see at this level. When I got ahead two balls and a strike, I threw the BrownBomber at a fastball and poked it into center for a legitimate base hit against a legit pitcher. He is the hardest thrower I've faced yet in four camps this side of Zane Smith and El Duque who once threw baseballs for big paychecks.

That base hit was the highlight of my day, which took an immediate turn for the worse when I realized the BrownBomber cracked on contact with the Dunlap fastball. Even though it was the epitome of a broken bat base hit, I was now two bats down and very sad.

A new bat, a walk, and force out later, the game moved to the seventh inning and we were tied at 2–2. Not many camp games total only four runs scored in six innings. We started the top of the seventh with a leadoff walk and Blass put Dunlap back in after pitching him only the first two innings. Campers are maxed at three innings pitched in a game. Dunlap strikes out the first guy he sees, then shortstop Rowley got a clean hit to left to put runners on first and third with one out. The potential game-winning run was on my shoulders, and I was using a bat I hadn't had a chance to bond with yet and was not at all comfortable with. A walk sounded very appealing. After falling behind 0–2 with the odds stacked against me and giving up twenty plus years, I was able to foul off the next two. By this time Dunlap was the hardest thrower I'd ever faced, including the ex-major leaguers in the respective Legends games.

Someone in the know told me afterwards he was throwing in the high seventies or low eighties, and frankly, that's out of my league. The next pitch was the hardest fastball I've ever seen, clearly inside, but became one of those fantasy camp, fantasy strikes and I got punched out. I caught myself before saying something to the umpire I would have regretted. With only nine guys and everyone having to play every inning, there was no room for back talk, and frankly, I was over-matched by the guy to begin with.

We stranded the runner at third, and now had to try and escape the heart of the Blass-Maz batting order in the bottom of the seventh. Their leadoff hitter, John Snodgrass, had only two hits in ten at-bats and appeared to be an easy start for us, but Snodgrass came up to the plate "convinced I was going to be the winning run."

He hit a windblown drive that found a hole in left-center, and he rounded first knowing it would be close at second. Snodgrass sensed a headfirst dive might be the only chance he had to make it, but he started his dive too early and wound up about a foot from the bag. In baseball terms, he "velcroed" it. "I felt like the ground grabbed me, like a fish on dry land," he laughed. On his hands and knees, he crawled to the base and got the benefit of the safe call from a compassionate umpire. However, he couldn't get back up.

Snodgrass, fifty-six, retired, and living outside Steubenville, Ohio, literally threw caution and his health to the wind for a fantasy camp win. As he slid, he momentarily forgot all about the six heart bypasses he had a decade ago, the four stents since, and his blood cancer which has been in remission for a year. Not to mention he is a severe diabetic. A win was a win, and his team needed it to make the playoffs.

The training staff helped Snodgrass up and off the field to the waiting medical cart. The next hitter, Dean Kajouras, fifty, had already doubled and tripled earlier in the game. I pleaded with coach Don Robinson to walk him, but Donnie paid no attention to me. Pirates manager Clint Hurdle was standing close by first base, laughing. I'm not sure what he was doing there, but clearly he wasn't scouting. We proceeded to strike Kajouras out. Hurdle smiled at me and I asked, "What would you have done?" He replied, "It doesn't matter what I would have done, I already told you guys that you know more than me." Ouch!

Our undefeated string lasted one more batter as a clean single to left by Eddie Morganstein, fifty-four, knocked in the pinch runner while Snodgrass was on his way to Manatee Memorial Hospital. We went as far as we could on fumes and were beaten 3–2 for our first loss of the week.

Snodgrass was diagnosed with a broken left arm and a detached rotator cuff. He got credit for the winning run just like he had envisioned on his way to the plate, sans the hospital visit.

Despite another very clean day in the field, I was disappointed in myself for not knocking in the runner in the seventh. For the life of me, at my age, I can't understand why I feel that way. Maybe there is still some competitive juice left in the tank after all. Still, with the afternoon free and guys scattering to the beaches, golf course, and card games, I considered heading downstairs to the batting cage. My legs advised otherwise.

We are all beaten up by now yet still have a doubleheader on Wednesday and at least one playoff round on Thursday. Just as I did the first time I was here, I literally had to pick up my legs with my arms to get in and out of bed last night and this morning. It becomes compounded when you realize you can't even sit out an inning or two because there's no one to replace you. Then reality sets in—you are paying big bucks for this experience, so shut up, take the pain, and have fun.

I prepared for this camp just as I did a year ago for the Yankees by visiting the teaching academy not far from home that's run by former major league infielder Jarrod Patterson.

We spent an hour together each session over four weeks throwing, catching ground balls, and then getting into the batting cage. There is no question, based upon going into my first camp in 2010 with no training, that I'm better for the experience. JP takes full credit for my fourteen for twenty-eight with the Yankees last year and fully expects to be thrown under the bus if things go south in this camp.

The highlight of my training sessions with JP would be when we finished and the next lesson on his schedule arrived. It's an eight- or maybe ten-year-old boy, and to see the look on the face of his dad as I'm wrapping up is priceless.

As I was finishing my final training session last week the kid's dad said, "Mind if I ask you a question?" I knew this guy had to be thinking, *Who is this guy and why on earth would he be doing this?* But instead, "I've seen you here often; are you an ex-pro trying to stay in shape?" I was about to tell him, "I'll have whatever you're having," but instead I told him the truth: "No. But I did stay at a Holiday Inn Express."

Wednesday

It was a beautiful sunny day on the west coast of Florida when the alarm rang at six o'clock, and I actually bounced out of bed. I didn't need to pick my legs up with my hands; my legs did it all by themselves.

I went down to an early breakfast and sitting alone was Law, who asked me to join him. They don't call this fantasy camp for nothing. I could listen all day to stories about the 1960 World Series, as I saw it happen through the eyes of an eight-year-old child. This morning he reflected on how everyone thought the Yankees would destroy the Pirates in that World Series. Everyone, he revealed, but the twenty-five guys who wore the Pirates uniform.

I had a feeling this was as good as the day was going to get and I wasn't wrong.

The woes continued for the beat-up Traynors. We dropped both games to run our losing streak to three after winning our first three. Suddenly the gang that couldn't lose a game became the gang that couldn't win one. To say we unraveled like a cheap suit would be unfair to the haberdashery industry.

Our stout nine survivors opened the day against a 2–2 team coached by former pitcher John "Candy" Candelaria and infielder Dave Cash. Candelaria, fifty-nine, was an intimidating 6'7" lefty with 177 wins over an eighteen-year career with eight teams. He was a 1977 All-Star, a 1979 World Champion with the Pirates, and the 1986 American League Comeback Player of the Year. He looked as if he could still bring it. We had a lot of time to chat during the 17–4 thrashing they laid upon us.

For the afternoon game, the temps moved into the low eighties, the winds blew over twenty mph, and the quads tightened. We were paired up against the other division leaders with a record of four wins and a loss, coached by former pitcher Zane Smith and catcher Manny Sanguillen. Sanguillen is a funny guy who still struggles with his broken English. This morning at kangaroo court, he wanted to honor one of his players who went "5 for 4" on Tuesday. Blass had some fun with that one.

We fell behind early and tried to come off the mat only to lose 9–5 and evened out our once perfect record at 3–3. Smith, fifty-one, is a delightful guy and coached first. He was here three years ago during my last visit. He won 100 big league games and is now living in Atlanta. Zane recently resurrected the Atlanta Braves fantasy camp. That was his goal in 2010 and they just finished their second year with about seventy campers.

As a team, we became flat and uninspired, which also described my day at the plate, the worst camp day in four years with a 1–6 and an RBI. I'd love to blame the day on TheBat and the BrownBomber being gone, or even instructor Jarrod Patterson, but the truth is, after seeing nothing but heat yesterday from a former Division 1 college pitcher, today seemed more like a slow-pitch softball game, and I just couldn't get in the groove. Bat or no bat, I was just lost. I will take a lesson from my wife's book here. On the rare occasion she has a bad day on the tennis court, Andi will come home and tell me, "I don't think I jeopardized my shoe contract." Amen, dear.

The good news is TheGlove continues to do its job, game in and game out.

We finished round robin league play at three up and three down. It was good enough to give us first place in our division by tiebreaker since we had beaten the other 3–3 team. As division champs, we move into the playoff round tomorrow as a very weak co-top seed. In fact, camp veterans cannot remember a time when a team won their first three games then lost the next three yet still had a record good enough to claim the division title. There are two semi-final games in the morning, with the winners playing for the camp championship in the afternoon. Sports books in Vegas are not taking much action on us.

Tomorrow is forecasted to be chilly for the one-day, two-round playoffs. We need to find the same magic we had on Sunday and Monday, when we were healthy, if we have any plans to advance. We open against the Blass-Mazeroski team that beat us 3–2 yesterday.

Thursday

I had no idea what a hip flexor was prior to this morning. Now I'm the proud owner of a strained one.

I knew it was something A-Rod would reinjure every August and excuse himself from hitting in the clutch for the rest of the season. I knew the mention of a hip flexor injury would make every Yankees fan cringe and boo wholeheartedly whenever #13 would return to the dugout hitless.

During my lackluster day at the plate yesterday, every time I tried to turn into the ball my right hip would be in pain. I thought nothing of it other than it's another area I need to ice after the doubleheader. The problem was when I went to put my pants on, I had to hold onto a chair or table to lift my right leg. I finally bit the bullet and went to the training room. I was training-room-free with the Tigers and Yankees, but the odds finally caught up with me.

The staff asked me to lie on a table. The trainer lifted my right leg. I screamed. He told me now I know what a hip flexor strain feels like. I was a little disappointed; I hoped it was a tweaked groin muscle. A tweaked groin muscle is the kind of injury that brings about mixed emotions: you hate that you tweaked the groin, but at sixty years of age, it's nice to know you still have one to tweak. I was down on the training table for about fifteen minutes with just about the hottest compress I've ever felt. When I took it off I could walk rather freely again, but when I went to put my uniform on, I still needed to brace myself.

With nine able bodies and the first round of the playoffs ninety minutes away, there was no room to even think about going on the disabled list. We needed everyone, and nearly all have some bruises, bumps, and limps, not only on our team but throughout camp.

Team Cuyler, the Blass-Mazeroski squad that ended our three-game winning streak, awaited. Predictably, their hard-throwing ace Dunlap took the mound again this morning. We had to be huge underdogs, having lost three in a row while the other guys rolled along with a 5–1 record.

For all practical purposes, this one was over in the top of the first. The Cuylers gave Dunlap an early 3–0 lead and that was enough as we did a poor job defensively and also ran ourselves out of a couple of innings. We were eliminated by a 5–2 score, far closer than it should have been. The once hottest team in camp finished by losing four straight games and concluded with a disappointing 3–4 overall record and a collapse for the camp record books.

Today's highlight was having Mazeroski coach first base and the constant chat throughout the game. We actually know some people in common through his winter golf exploits in the Florida panhandle. The sun was shining, though the temps dropped into the high sixties; fortunately for me, the wind was blowing briskly to the right. Maz is never without a cigar in his mouth, and the wind blowing away from me helped limit my morning emphysema risk.

Maz is a legend not only in Pittsburgh, but the Pirates fantasy camp uses him, rightly so, as their marquee name and attraction. He's been doing this for years. I asked him if he still enjoyed it. He didn't miss a beat. "Sure do. You get to see a lot of strange things in the course of a week."

That was the perfect entrée for me to tell him about my plans for this book and ask if he would contribute a few words. Modestly he said he had "nothing to add," but after a short chat, he agreed. I still shake my head, 1960s' style, that Maz would do something like this for the once eight-year-old kid from Long Island.

After struggling with my hip, I was justifiably dropped to eighth in the order this morning and batted only twice in a low-scoring, fast-paced game with a ground out and walk. While I still miss my two busted bats, I was pleased I could stand upright for all seven innings in the field.

As a spectator to the afternoon championship game, the temps sharply dropped to the low sixties and the Cuyler team easily won the camp title to no one's surprise with a convincing 11–4 win over the team coached by Richie Hebner and Bob Walk, a team we routed 9–1 earlier in the week when we were still good and I could hit. John Snodgrass was released from the hospital with his arm and shoulder in a cast and sling in time for the trophy ceremony.

All that's left for us now is the Legends game on Friday against the former major leaguers. Everyone gets to take at least one at-bat against a big league pitcher and play an inning or two in the field.

Coaches LaValliere and Robinson gathered us together after we got knocked out and LaValliere said, "I had such a great week with you guys, it was so much fun," but he had to get one more coaching dig in. "Today you saw why baseball is a game of three outs. If you give them four or five outs the way you guys did, you'll get beat every time. In closing," Spanky said, "we play against you guys in the morning, so screw all of you."

The empathy and respect we had for Don Robinson this week was amazing, unspeakable, and really unthinkable. Don, a 109-game winner in the bigs, had the worst possible thing happen to him less than a month before camp. His thirty-year-old son Brent, Brent's wife Julie, and her parents were among five people killed in a terrible automobile accident in Kentucky on Christmas Eve.

I'm really not sure how someone gets through such a tragedy, especially with so little time having passed since the horrible incident. Perhaps Don needed the distraction of camp to keep his mind on other things and not a word was said about it publicly all week. For someone like me who has everything he wants in life, including good family health, this tragedy is unimaginable. My respect for Don Robinson is immense and we hope he and his family are coping the best they can with a situation that is as bad as it can be. It was nice to see the LaValliere-Robinson friendship at work and the comfort they gave each other.

Friday

Every camp has the guy who feels he has to make some noise. Either he thinks he's playing in the seventh game of the World Series or has a free agent contract riding on his statistics. The guy who will put on the eye-black and wear some bling and go hard into second base to break up a double play. In many ways, this week has become their life and that's not the intent or spirit of camp. Fortunately, they are few and far between, but normally they stick out on the first day of camp.

And then there's Reverend John Zingaro, fifty-eight, who is competing at his sixth Pirates camp. He fully understands it might be his last.

The "Rev," as he is known around Pirate City, is by trade a Presbyterian pastor. He seemingly fought a successful battle against colon cancer in 2006 following his second Pirates camp, which originally was gifted to him by his congregation outside of Madison, Wisconsin. Even though he was based in Milwaukee Brewers country, Rev was born an hour outside of Pittsburgh in Ellwood City, Pennsylvania, and never compromised his Pirates allegiance. When camp ended seven years ago, he had surgery followed by six months of chemotherapy, which successfully put the illness into remission.

While he missed 2007 fantasy camp, he returned in 2008 and again in 2010. A year ago, following the 2012 camp, Rev went for a routine blood test in Peoria, Illinois, where he was serving a congregation. He was jolted to learn the cancer had returned. Some of the colon cancer cells had gotten into his lymph nodes. The chemotherapy treatment in 2006 didn't get it all and it wasn't until six years later that the cancer cells massed enough to be detected during a routine blood test. This time the cancer had metastasized to his abdomen and was much worse. Stage IV. Nine months of chemotherapy followed, only to prove ineffective. Still, Rev did not know how dire his situation was until he met with the oncologist in Peoria in October 2012.

"The doctor told me the treatment was not working, there was no known cure for this type of cancer, and this wasn't an illness that would kill me in five or ten years," the Reverend said. "He told me this illness would kill me soon."

Rev left Peoria and moved back to Pittsburgh two months later to be with his family during what he worried would be his last days. He arranged to see a specialist at the famed Hillman Cancer Center in Pittsburgh, and in early January a CAT scan revealed the cancer was still growing. He was referred to the best hands he could find as surgery was imminent.

When Rev heard this, not knowing when the surgery would be scheduled, he quickly spoke up. "I have plans to go to Florida at the end of the month."

The Hillman Cancer Center oncologist smiled and said, "Good. Go down there and lie in the sun. That'll be good for you."

Rev replied, "I'm not going there to lie in the sun. I'm going to Florida to play baseball."

The day before flying to this camp, the Rev met his surgeon, Dr. Dave Bartlett, a pioneer in operating on the advanced type of abdominal cancer that was supposedly incurable. The surgeon is also an avid Pirates fan.

The surgery was scheduled for March 1. Dr. Bartlett told Rev, "We won't know what can be done until we get in there, but try and enjoy your week and please take it easy." Rev arrived at Pirate City harboring this renewed uncertainly about his life. Only four months earlier, he literally had begun mulling over music for his funeral. Still, he was determined to come to camp this week. "I didn't know if I would be alive next year, so there was no reason to delay," Rev said.

Cancer couldn't hold the Reverend back, and it's probably good that Dr. Bartlett didn't see Rev's idea of "taking it easy." He not only came to camp but he conquered it. "I was tired but I had a really good camp. Who's worried about a fastball when literally your life is on the line?" he said.

Incredibly, he hit .429, third highest on his team, playing like every at-bat was his last, and in his playoff game he had all three of the team's RBIs. To make matters even tougher, Rev is a catcher. Between the sometimes-scattered arms of camp pitchers and wearing the heavy catcher's armor, there's no such thing as "taking it easy." He caught just about every inning for Team Clemente, coached by Sanguillen and Smith.

"One of the important things for people with cancer is to try and do as much as you can for your morale, and that defines fantasy baseball camp," Rev said. "I wanted to come see my Pirates family, and I came here never knowing if I would be back again."

Amazingly, during the games you wouldn't know anything was wrong with Rev, and he wouldn't give you the first clue.

Every time you came to bat and he was crouched behind the plate, he would make small talk about your swing, your family, or a play you made in the field. "Class" falls short in defining this guy.

Then on March 1, 2013, a miracle happened. After a twelve-hour surgery at the Hillman Cancer Center, Dr. Bartlett removed multiple tumors from Rev's abdominal wall and a sizable tumor blocking his rectum. Rev lost fifty-five pounds and is still a bit slow getting around, sporting about a foot-long scar up his chest. Knowing recovery is only a matter of time, he's headed back to Bradenton in January, looking to strap on the catcher's tools and improve on his .429 average.

Reverend John Zingaro was pronounced cancer-free. Dr. Dave Bartlett has an autographed Bill Mazeroski baseball sitting on his mantel. Seems like a perfect ending!

Back to Friday morning. It's the last day of fantasy camp at Pirate City and a wrap for my fourth year of playing with other kids my age and beyond, and with some major leaguers I worshiped long ago.

The temps are chilly, in the forties, and the brisk weather greeted our early morning breakfast as we prepared for the rites of the final day: a chance for us campers to play a quick couple of innings against the Pirates Legends.

Sinking quicker than the real Pirates did in 2012, our team, the Traynors, wound up the overall fifth seed, despite being the top team in camp only three days earlier. With no endorsement contracts in jeopardy, this ultimately means we get to play the fifth game out of eight against the Legends.

The good news about playing the fifth game of the day was that it gave the temperature a chance to warm up, and by the time we hit the field it was into the mid-fifties. As a bonus, it gave the Legends a chance to grow even older.

As the designated home team, the top of the first began in intimidating style for me. The first two batters of the game were both lefties—the still-fleet-footed Omar Moreno, and the still-imposing Richie Hebner. The thought of the airport at that moment had great appeal. In the meantime, I tried to peer over to the Legends bench to see who might be throwing against us in the bottom of the inning.

Moreno walked and Hebner singled to center. It seemed a bit surreal as I tried to hold Hebner close to the base. As Hebner took a lead, he asked me, "How did that swing tip I gave you work out?" I told him he got to see the best shot I hit all week and thanked him once again for the swing and the memory it provided.

Three runs scored by the Legends ended an inning. The game normally goes two or three innings, so every camper gets a chance to bat. On a bad day, it takes the Legends about five batters to score three runs; this morning, only four.

Zane Smith pitched the early games for the Legends, so I figured we would not face him. That was fine by me, as Zane was the first major leaguer I ever batted against back in 2010. The likely candidates were John Candelaria or Bob Walk. Facing a 6'7" lefty like Candy didn't start my motor.

Walk, who has a terrible name for a pitcher, was the designee to face us. Bob, fifty-six, had 105 wins in a thirteen-year career divided between the Pirates, Braves, and Phillies. He won a World

Series ring with the Phillies in 1980 and was an All-Star with the Pirates in 1988.

He didn't seem particularly shaken by the prospect of facing me, and I flew out to left on a 1–1 fastball. I wasn't disappointed at all by the at-bat. Of the four ex-big leaguers I have faced—Smith and El Duque Hernandez, both infield ground outs, and Frank Tanana, an infield broken bat single where the bat went further than the ball—today was the best contact I'd made. Chalk one up for the fantasy camp memories.

Saturday

A month or so ago, I doubted things would happen the way they did this week.

During my first Birmingham training session with JP in early January, I couldn't throw the ball. Literally. I couldn't throw it, and whenever I tried, I was in pain. Strangely, I could swing the bat pain-free, but I couldn't throw and was questioning whether I could make it here or not.

I found out it was a triceps bruise, so I did what all world-class athletes do and contacted Dr. James Andrews.

Luckily, Dr. Andrews, the foremost doctor in the world for sports orthopedics, is a Birmingham resident and a member of my company's advisory board. Dr. Andrews is unquestionably the orthopedic surgeon to the stars. Among the thousands and thousands of athletes from high school to the professional ranks that he has helped during their careers are names like Brett Favre, Tom Brady, Drew Brees, Albert Pujols, Michael Jordan, Jack Nicklaus, Roy Berger, Roger Clemens, Troy Aikman, Bo Jackson,

CC Sabathia, and Peyton Manning. Shall I go on? His prize patient this past season was Minnesota running back Adrian Peterson, his new knee and dead aim on the record book.

Except Doc Andrews wasn't having a great weekend himself. His patient, Robert Griffin III, went down with a severe knee injury, and Doc got caught in a round of "he said/she said" with the Washington Redskins coaching staff that played out on national television.

Timing may have never been my strong suit, but I contacted Dr. Andrews the day after RG3 went down and told him my story. He prefaced his advice with words you really don't want to hear. "At your age," Doc began. At my age? Anyway, he recommended icing the triceps daily, not throwing for a few days, taking Aleve and using IcyHot to relieve any discomfort. I was throwing again by the following Friday, and while I won't gun a runner down going from second to third, it's sure nice knowing at least I got the ball back to the pitcher.

In thanking Doc, I asked him if he wanted a signed picture of #60 of the Pittsburgh Pirates fantasy camp for his photo wall of accomplished patients. He told me he'd get back to me.

A tricep strain. A hip flexor injury. A four-year low batting average—turning sixty is a bitch.

That about sums up my fantasy week: bumps, bruises, frustration at the plate due to injury, and getting old.

Despite it all, it was a wonderful week.

Pittsburgh Pirates fantasy camp 2013 was almost as good as the 2010 original for me. Three years ago I was a bright-eyed and very unsuspecting rookie. I returned as a seasoned veteran with two other camp experiences sandwiched in between, the excitement and thrill of newfound discovery replaced by realistic expectations.

If you like the idea of putting on a baseball uniform every day, this is an experience you should not miss. There is something mysterious and romantic and liberating to walk around in baseball togs fifty years after you have license to do so.

I wrapped up my week and headed home. Off the field, it's time to get back to the family and to the office. On the field, the week was so-so for me. I didn't perform the way I had expected, and part of that is due to an injury or two, part is age, and part is attrition of our team which forced everyone remaining to play every inning of every game.

For the previous three camps, my baseball cards claim I was twenty-eight for fifty-six for a pretty nifty .500 "career" camp batting average. Things went south this week, and other than the blast to the 335 sign in right field, my numbers were a bit sub-par for camp and my expectations. I finished the week with seven hits in twenty at-bats for a .350 average with six RBIs, two runs scored, five walks, and a pretty cool double; if I had it to do over again, I would have headed for third.

While my epitaph will never be "he was a great guy," perhaps it can be "he hit for a career .461 in fantasy camp baseball."

I was really proud of my glove this week. It played over fifty innings in the field with just about as many chances and was errorless. First base in adult Little League is not easy. Very few third basemen can make the throw all the way across the diamond; shortstops and second basemen can be iffy as well. You spend more time on your knees than a carpet installer and try your best to help your infielders look good. Then you have to factor in the angle of the sun, which at times, especially in the afternoon, can be blinding. I am proud of my week and TheGlove.

The Traynors, while never as good as our starting 3–0 record, weren't as bad as our 0–4 finish. It's interesting to see a group of guys mesh both on and off the field when put together for a week, and once again, it happened at this camp. If fantasy camp resembles reality in any way, then we collapsed—just as the real Pirates did last season. I hate when that happens.

Twelve guys started and three were quickly lost to injury, but everyone stayed with the program and tried their best to contribute. Some of the injured guys made all-out efforts that would make any medical professional wince. The average age of our team was fifty-three, just shy of the average camp age, with our oldest at sixty-three and our youngest at forty-five. For once it felt good not being the oldest in a group, although some days it sure felt that way.

And our coaches for the week—catcher Spanky LaValliere and pitcher Don Robinson—were true delights who looked out for our best interests despite the cloud hanging over Mr. Robinson. I have to say, in all four camp experiences the pro staffing has been very similar: approachable, engaging, and most of them wanting to win. They are paid an average $2,500 a week and I still can't tell if it's tough work for them, a week's worth of giggles, or something in between.

It's time to wind it down and find some salve. Four years of fantasy camps and the aches and pains of this year in particular tell me time it's time to hang up the glove and find something a bit safer and less painful to do, but I don't want to stop. The reality is that my body may be telling me it's time. It's a great week every year and something I would truly miss.

Excuse me for a minute. I have to send in my deposit for next year.

Wearing #60 and taking aim at the 335-foot sign in right.

Meeting one of my 1960 idols—Elroy Face.

The Pirates training staff preparing for another busy camp day.

Mike "Spanky" LaValliere and Don Robinson encourage us to stop losing.

Vern Law talking 1960 World Series at early morning coffee.

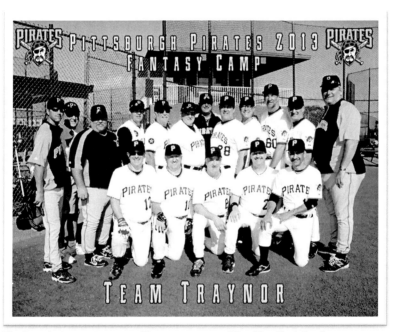

The best 3–4 team in camp. Pirates manager Clint Hurdle is back row center.

Eighth Inning

Where's Rudy Hernandez?

March 2013

*S*ixty days after Pirates camp ended, I was on the operating table for an arthroscopic procedure to correct something called Impingement Syndrome. We non-medical types know it as cleaning out bone chips and spurs in the shoulder joint.

The hip flexor healed in about a week with heat and time. The ice and Aleve that Dr. Andrews recommended as a palliative measure for the strained triceps to get me through camp eased, but once home I still felt considerable left shoulder pain. I went to see a colleague, Dr. Kenneth Bramlett, who, after X-rays and discussing my camp throwing discomfort, asked me a series of questions:

Dr. B: Do you have pain when swinging a golf club? Yes.

Dr. B: Do you have pain when putting on a seat belt? Yes.

Dr. B: Do you have pain when putting on your jacket? Yes.

Dr. B: Do you have pain when combing your hair? What hair?

Dr. B: Are you having discomfort sleeping at night? Big time.

Dr. B: Can you make the throw to third base? Are you nuts?

The diagnosis was simple. He gave me a steroid shot to ease my pain. I yelped. He called me "candy-ass" and put me through some exercises that ruled out a rotator cuff problem and determined it was the more patient-friendly diagnosis of bone spurs. He said I could keep coming back for shots, though he recommended outpatient surgery and promised it wouldn't have me immobile for more than a day or two. That seemed to be the only solution.

The injury had nothing to do with baseball, but was more likely caused from years of lugging a carry-on suitcase through airports and hotels as I built frequent flyer and hotel loyalty points plus the office briefcase that was strapped over my shoulder a couple of times a day.

The chance to be free of pain when I put on a jacket or reached to tuck in my shirt or have Ibis fling back my arm while playing was enough for me to get it taken care of. Swinging a golf club over twenty-five or thirty rounds a year and throwing a baseball each January was only the frosting on the healthy shoulder cake.

Playing baseball over the last four years gave me plenty of time to think about my attraction to the game. Your special interest fabric is cast at a very young age. Through the years it gets molded, amended, modified, added to, deleted from. There's always a part of our childhood that makes the long life journey with us.

For me it is sports, and particularly baseball, for as long as I can remember. The memories sharpen and the picture becomes more vivid beginning with the 1960 World Series and traveling through time. I'm not sure what it is about baseball that captivates me.

I flirted with hockey, football, and basketball and still love those games, but there is something about baseball that never left me. It seems romantic in a very strange way. Grown men wearing silly uniforms that don't fit. Coaches and managers wearing the same uniform, a fact no one has an explanation for other than offering, "That's the way it's always been." What amazed me from the first time I realized it, is baseball is the only game where the ball is not in control of the offense. The defense controls the ball and you have to literally flip it into play to put them on defense. It's the only sport constructed like that. Cricket doesn't count.

With the best moment of my young life sealed safely in my mind with the 1960 Pittsburgh Pirates World Championship, I didn't actually see my first major league game in person until the next season when Dad surprised me for my birthday.

Dad grew up in upper Manhattan in a very nice part of the city known as Washington Heights, which was primarily Jewish and Italian back in the forties and fifties but was developing a Hispanic flair. He was friendly from both his neighborhood and George Washington High School with a guy two years his junior born in the Dominican Republic named Rudy Hernandez. They were both very tall for those days, 6'3", and Rudy happened to possess a right arm that got him to the big leagues as the first Dominican-born pitcher, preceding the great Juan Marichal by sixteen days.

Hernandez made his major league debut in 1960 for the Washington Senators, and for my ninth birthday in 1961, Dad gave me a postcard from Rudy Hernandez. It was the real deal, too. He was pictured in his Senators uniform and posed in pitching stance on the back. Inscribed on the front was, *"Herb, look forward to helping celebrate your son's birthday when we come to New York on May 17. I will take him to the locker room after the game."* Are you kidding me? Going into a major league locker room at nine years old. It wasn't the Pirates, but it just might have been the second greatest day of my life. And my dad actually did know a real baseball player.

May 17, 1961, eleven days past my ninth birthday, seems like yesterday. We walked into Yankee Stadium for the very first time. We bought a game program for fifteen cents. We went up the portal on the third base side. My first sight was a mass of green. The outfield was so pretty and immaculately manicured. I had never seen that much green grass in my life. I opened the scorecard and searched for Rudy Hernandez's name and #23, his number. There was no Rudy Hernandez or #23 listed.

Getting around Yankee Stadium that day wasn't particularly difficult with only 6,200 people in attendance, but the only one that mattered to me we couldn't find. Hernandez was a relief pitcher, so we hurried to the Washington bullpen located down the left field line, which was very accessible. My dad leaned over and asked one of the Senators, "Where's Rudy Hernandez?" The response still chills me. "He got sent down to the minors a week ago."

I hadn't been kicked in the gut before that day. Now I knew what it felt like. Hernandez was shipped to AAA, first Toronto, then Indianapolis, after appearing in only seven games with the

Senators and giving up eight hits. We stayed for the rest of the game. Washington won 8–7. Roger Maris hit one of his sixty-one home runs. I didn't care. It quickly turned into the worst day of my life.

About a week later, another Rudy Hernandez postcard arrived in the mail. *"Herb—Sorry I wasn't with the club in NY but baseball is a funny game. I'll be back up there soon and I'll sure keep my promise to your son."* Sadly for both of us, Hernandez never made it back to the big leagues and I never made it to the locker room. At the time, I didn't think baseball was a very funny game at all.

Fortunately, Herb Berger had a longer career than his good pal Rudy Hernandez. Dad was never sent down to the minors but instead worked very hard providing for a family of five in the wholesale fish business at the Fulton Fish Market. New Amsterdam Seafood was a purveyor to most of New York's top restaurants, clubs, and hotels, and Dad put the three of us through college while Mom stayed home and picked up after her sons. I'm still not sure who worked harder.

Being a Pirates fan, I was a National League kid and NL baseball returned to New York in 1962. Well, sort of. The 1962 expansion New York Mets, despite sporting the colors of their predecessors—orange for the Giants and blue for the Dodgers—were perhaps the worst team to ever play the game. The "Amazins," as they were known for their amazing ability to screw up any situation, set a major league record for futility by losing 120 of the 160 games they played in 1962, finishing "only" sixty games behind the pennant-winning San Francisco Giants. Mets manager Casey Stengel asked that season, "Can't anyone around here play this game?" It's a cry you can hear almost daily at fantasy camp.

The Mets had a lavish new stadium being built for them in Queens, but it was still a couple of years away from completion, so they played in the Polo Grounds, abandoned by the Giants when they left New York for San Francisco after the 1957 season. The Polo Grounds also had another tenant in the fledgling American Football League with the New York Titans who also moved to Queens in 1964 and changed their name to the Jets in homage to neighboring LaGuardia Airport.

The Polo Grounds was outdated even in 1962. Narrow around the corners, about 260 feet down the lines and 483 feet deep in the middle, it was shaped a bit like a bathtub and gave Willie Mays all the room he needed to make his circus over-the-shoulder catch in the 1954 World Series against Cleveland. Oddly, both team clubhouses were also located in center field, which made for a very long walk at game's end.

My first Polo Grounds experience was in the summer of 1962 on a long-forgotten date against a long-forgotten opponent, but I know it wasn't the Pirates. Dad and I were joined by some friends from Long Island and their sons, and of the two memories I take from my National League debut, one was the ability to see Yankee Stadium over the left-center field wall. I couldn't believe you could sit in one major league stadium and see another. The Polo Grounds was on the upper west side of Manhattan and just across the Harlem River was the Bronx and the façade of Yankee Stadium. From inside Yankee Stadium you couldn't see the Polo Grounds, but with the wide, outfield expanse of the Polo Grounds, you could clearly see the stadium with its famed frieze and marquee. It's the last time in baseball history that ever happened.

218

I also remember leaving the game that day. Outside, under the elevated train tracks and waiting for the light to change, was Roy Campanella. Campy was a great catcher for the Dodgers in the fifties who was paralyzed in a terrible automobile accident in 1958. Immobile from the shoulders down, he sat waiting for the light to change in his wheelchair and I told Dad I wanted to get his autograph. My father gently explained to me why that was impossible. I did go over and say hello.

Two years later, in an area known as Flushing Meadows, the World's Fair began in Queens. With it was the opening of the Mets' and Jets' new home, Shea Stadium, named after William Shea, who was instrumental in bringing National League baseball back to New York after the Dodgers and Giants left for California.

Shea became a regular stop for me over the next six years through high school. With little traffic, it was only about thirty minutes from home. Regularly, my high school buddy T. Santolli and I lead an entourage to the games, or just the two of us would go. Seeing the Pirates every year as much as I could was a foregone conclusion.

In 1964, Shea was perhaps the most magnificent place you would ever imagine, but it soon took a back seat to the cookie-cutter ovals of cement-style ballparks of the same ilk in Philadelphia, Pittsburgh, Cincinnati, St. Louis, and Atlanta. Of all the days spent at Shea, two experiences stand out.

Tuesday, June 27, 1967, and the Pirates were in town. We had great seats behind the plate. Before the game, a scene for the movie *The Odd Couple* was shot.

The movie premise was, "The greatest play in Mets history missed by sportswriter Oscar Madison." Still known as habitual losers, in the script, the Mets had a one-run lead in the top of the ninth and the Pirates had the bases loaded, nobody out, and Bill Mazeroski at-bat. Just as Mets pitcher Jack Fisher gets ready to release the ball, Madison (Walter Matthau), the schlep sports writer, gets called away to the phone by his roommate, the overly-tidy and neurotic Felix Unger (Jack Lemmon) who tells him he is at the supermarket and wants to know what to buy for dinner. Of course, while the phone call is taking place, Maz bounces into an incredible triple play to end the game for the best win in Mets history. Oscar, out of the press box, is literally left holding the phone.

Rumor had it that Roberto Clemente was originally offered the batter's role (and the whopping $100 that went with it), but he had too much pride to seem "weak" at-bat and turned it down. Maz, still a top-shelf name, accepted the spot and it only took only two or three takes to shoot the scene. Clemente might have been on to something as the Pirates also lost the real game that night, 5–2. Two years later those hapless Mets were World Champions.

Funny, but with all the time spent with Maz at Pirates camp, I never thought of asking him about that day. It's now on my checklist of things to do.

Many years, many ballparks, and a loyalty change to Yankees pinstripes came between that day in 1967 and my second great Shea Stadium memory on October 26, 2000. It was Game 5 of the World Series between the Mets and Yankees. We had no way of knowing that less than eleven months later and only ten or so miles away, our quasi-secure world as we thought we knew it would perish forever.

The 2000 World Series brought out the spirit of New York with the city torn between the Mets and the Yankees. The Yankees won the Series 4–1 and I was at the clincher with my brother Ken, an over-the-top Mets fan and Yankees hater, which was the worse combination for him that night. He would not stay for the completion of the bottom of the ninth because, "I don't want to watch THEM celebrate on our field," so as Mariano Rivera got Mike Piazza to fly out to Bernie Williams and win the Series, I tossed my cap in the air in the parking lot while the Yankees fans went crazy in the stadium.

Sixty years later on July 24, 2012, I came full circle and saw my first Pirates home game. Never making it to Forbes Field is one of my great sports regrets. I envisioned the stadium as a kid over and over but never got there in person. Forbes Field was demolished in 1971 and the Pirates moved to Three Rivers Stadium, which, other than the tenant, had no appeal. I was able to get some Forbes Field fix in later years as the original left field wall and home plate still stand on the University of Pittsburgh campus in approximately the same place as when it was a ball field. For me it was at least a little taste.

Pirates camp director Joe Billetdeaux asked me to be his guest for my long overdue Pittsburgh debut at PNC Park, as pretty a place as everyone says. The backdrop of downtown Pittsburgh over right-center field is stunning. The Pirates proceeded to drop a 5–1 sleeper to the Cubs that night, and Billetdeaux said it was okay with him if I waited another sixty years before I came back.

So much baseball since 1960, and still today when I get a chance I can sit for hours and watch the Yankees. The day-to-day novelty as a kid has been cashed in for the responsibilities of life, but on a daily basis, I know how the Yankees did, how the Red Sox made out, and cast an eye for the Pirates score and that elusive winning season.

Year in and year out baseball results may have become foggy with time, but the personal highlights are still so sharp in my mind. The chance to get on the field and be a major leaguer, long gone in thought, has been my catalyst that truly you can still do almost anything you want in life if you are blessed with health. This experience that began in 2010 has lit a fire inside me that burns brighter and stronger today than it did the day before camp initially started in 2010. It's very hard to describe when fantasy becomes reality. Or as I was so astutely told early on in the process, "Fantasy camp is like a drug, you'll see."

I always believed age was nothing more than a chronological number, but once I turned sixty I realized how wrong I had been. Simultaneously things started to go when I hit sixty. I felt a keen loss of energy at certain times during the day; physically, my early morning workouts became tougher, but it's a way of life and I need to do it, if for nothing else, the mental stimulation. The desire to travel, go to events, and generally socialize outside of necessary business networks hit the skids. Even the Red Sox and Florida Gators winning doesn't bother me the way it used to. Are you thinking what I am? Potential to be a walking billboard for 5-hour Energy? And strangely, it all happened almost to the clock of turning sixty. Thus hitting a baseball, while never easy, felt the calendar, too.

I know the end of this chapter in my life is near. It became more difficult to keep the engine running this time around. If I hang up the uniform and checkbook for good, I won't go without an emotional struggle and there will be a big void that will need to be filled with something else. I guess I could go look for Rudy Hernandez or perhaps try and resurrect my failed stand-up comedy career which washed out in 2007 after eight poor sets in Birmingham and Atlanta. More than likely, I would pursue what really interests me—secondary- or college-level teaching. I might be good at public relations, marketing, or general business courses and could rely on years of practical experience. I'm just not sure what school would be looking for a 6′3″, 205-pound, left-handed professor with a career lifetime fantasy camp batting average of .461.

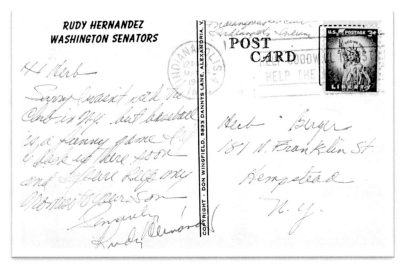

The crushing 1961 postcard from Rudy Hernandez.

Explaining to my comedic idol, Don Rickles, how my stand-up
career went so wrong.

Ninth Inning

Forty Years Later

June 2013

*E*ight weeks after shoulder surgery and forty years later than originally contemplated, there I stood: at first base in my Pittsburgh Pirates white uniform at PNC Park, home of the Bucs.

I'm sure I envisioned this day happening, but that was back in the early 1960s and long forgotten. About the time my lack of ability became obvious, was just about the same time my major league dreams faded away. Until June 1, 2013, when it finally happened!

In my mind's eye a half century ago, I stood at first base in the then-Pirates home, Forbes Field. In my youthful imagination, I looked around—sharing the infield with me was Don Hoak, Dick Groat, and Bill Mazeroski. As I glanced over my right shoulder, I could see Bob Skinner in left, Bill Virdon in center, and then with goose bumps realized Roberto Clemente was behind me in right field. On the mound was Cy Young Award-winner Vernon Law throwing to catcher Smoky Burgess. In the dugout pulling all the right strings was manager Danny Murtaugh.

This morning I looked around the infield and saw Brent McCall, Gary Dmitrzak, and Jay DeLuca, a retired steel worker, a corporate CFO, and architect, respectively. In the outfield was Dean DeLuca, Bill Diamondstone, and Greg Gasparich—a sales director, IT program manager, and restaurateur. The battery consisted of a dentist, Dr. Jim Forshey, and an undertaker, Dennis Hoover. In the dugout wasn't Danny Murtaugh but instead Todd Rowley, FBI Special Agent, who on this day was not only our best ballplayer but was on the DL and couldn't give it a go. We all had one thing in common—we were living our dream.

A nice little perk to being a Pirates fantasy camper is the annual Pirates-hosted "reunion game" in early June at PNC Park. The beauty that is PNC Park opened in 2001 on the same site, at the confluence of the Ohio, Allegheny, and Monongahela Rivers, as the aptly named Three Rivers Stadium, which hosted both the Pirates and the Pittsburgh Steelers. The PNC Park outfield opens to a stunning view of downtown Pittsburgh, right across the Roberto Clemente Bridge. It seats a very compact 38,362 baseball fans, who up until this season have never seen the Pirates play better than .500 baseball. Finally, as manager Clint Hurdle assured us at fantasy camp back in January, the Pirates ended the longest losing streak in professional sports in twenty years by winning their eighty-second game with a 1–0 victory over the Texas Rangers on September 9 to not only guarantee a winning season but miraculously also head to the post-season. The city rejoiced, the agony ended, and the Pirates battle cry of "Raise the Jolly Roger" could be heard throughout city of Pittsburgh for the first time since 1992!

I caught myself watching more and more Pirates games this year and pulled for them to stop the futility while also wondering how good Andrew McCutchen would look playing center field day in and day out in Yankee Stadium. The answer is really good.

It was six thirty a.m. on my major league morning and I'm finally ready to make my big league stadium debut forty years after I planned to be drafted by the Pirates. I was pretty certain back in 1965 that by my twenty-first birthday I would be signed, sealed, and headed to Pittsburgh. Andi opened the curtains in the Pittsburgh hotel overlooking PNC Park and said, "I hate to tell you this but it's raining." The three scheduled fantasy camp reunion games each last for one hour and had to end by eleven a.m. so the stadium crew could prepare for that evening's game when the real Pirates hosted the Reds. The hands of time nor the rain in the sky was working in our favor.

I jumped out of bed and took a look, and all I could think was "Lakeland" and the rain. Turned the TV on, and although the weatherman promised clearing skies, the first game started in ninety minutes and I was all too familiar with wet fields and cancellations from my week with the Tigers.

This time the worry was for naught. The rain stopped, the skies turned blue, and the baking sun brought big time humidity. The first game kicked off at eight a.m., right on time. Over seventy of the ninety-six January campers returned for their hour on the big stage, and coordinator Joe Billetdeaux did the best he could to keep the January teams together for the reunion games.

Our game was scheduled for nine a.m., and the excitement had me headed across the street to PNC Park in full uniform an hour early. I knew this was the real deal when the security guard waved me through a door that said, "Authorized Personnel Only," a sign that every sports fan has encountered on a stadium or arena visit and is known to indicate a sacred area that's taboo and off-limits. Not for me for one day.

I walked down a long corridor lined with pictures of great moments in Pirates history and another security-type invited me to enter what would be the campers' clubhouse for the morning, usually used as the umpires' dressing room. Quickly and excitedly, I changed into my baseball shoes, said a quick hello to some of the guys, and strode back down the hall. I made a left turn where the sign indicated "Pirates Players and Staff Only," walked straight ahead through the darkness of the tunnel into the Pirates dugout, and finally emerged onto the expansive beauty of PNC Park. For a giddy moment, I was that kid again!

While the early game was being played, I walked around the field to take it all in. Many of these guys play the reunion game year after year, but for this reunion game rookie it was a treat and one I was going to savor for every second.

It was a special moment when Reverend John Zingaro walked out on the field to say hello to the guys. Rev, with successful cancer surgery in the win column, might look a few pounds lighter, but his presence sure boosted everyone's spirits, and he plans to be back in uniform in Bradenton in January. A great story for a really good guy.

Ten of us from our January team, the Traynors, made it to the reunion. It was nice sharing the experience with those who have become friends during our week together. Two others, Dr. Jay Petruska and John Gasper, had date conflicts, and Rowley, the third FBI guy I had as a past camp teammate, was injured, which weakened us. The not-so-nice part was we were on a four game losing streak, though that was tempered somewhat when we found out we were playing the Stargells, losers of five of their seven games at camp. Something had to give.

We were the home team. There I stood on first base, a few minutes after nine a.m. I couldn't believe it; first base for the Pittsburgh Pirates. Dad, now eighty-four, was at home in South Florida with my ailing mom, but I believe he would have done anything he could to be there even if I was sixty-one years old and this was happening forty years behind schedule. Who cares? I was, for one hour, the first baseman for the Pittsburgh Pirates on their home field. I couldn't help but think about the October 13, 1960, celebratory hug Dad and I exchanged on our driveway.

I closed my eyes for a moment and through the din of the power washers cleaning the stadium seats behind me, envisioned playing in front of 38,362 fans; though on this day, only about 100 family and friends were in the stands. In reality, I was playing in a major league stadium with over 38,000 empty seats. I knew what it felt like to be a Miami Marlin.

To top off the experience, the first time I walked to the plate, Joe Klimchak of the Pirates public relations staff was the PA announcer. "Batting fifth and playing first base from Birmingham, Alabama, numba 56, Rrrroy Berrrrrgerrrrr." The only thing missing was my Lynyrd Skynyrd "Sweet Home Alabama" walk-up music.

That was as good as a great day can get. Our team didn't improve from January, and the bright stadium lights must have gotten to our infielders. What is normally a challenging job at first base digging stuff out of the dirt and catching balls that hop five feet in front of you and over your head was compounded today by guys with the jitters that resulted in tosses into the dugout, the stands, and one that actually struck the first base umpire on the wrist as he got ready to make a call. When it was over, the Stargells had extended our losing streak to five with a 1–0 five-inning win.

I got two PNC Park plate appearances and left there still looking for my first big league stadium hit. I was a lethargic 0–2 with two groundouts against camp veterans Ted Geletka and Kevin Kubala. I wanted to blame a healing shoulder, but truthfully, it was tougher thinking about the post-surgical pain than it was to swing the bat. Oh well, something to shoot for next year.

The exhilaration of the day didn't fade away quickly. In fact, I was still riding high for about a week after I got home, when a package was delivered from the Pirates. It was my 2013 Pirates baseball card, a memento that every camper anxiously awaits.

I clearly remember the excitement as a kid collecting baseball cards. You couldn't wait to rip open the pack, shed the hard, cavity-laden piece of bubble gum, and see "who you got." You then went right to the checklist to take another step in completing the set or hoped to have valuable collateral to try and trade with buddies.

I ripped open the Pirates envelope and was pleased to see a very nice picture of me in my Pirates black uniform, just having stroked the ball and running (or whatever it is I do these days) to first. Impressive. Then I flipped the card over. For as long as I can remember there was a player profile/biography on the back that we never read as kids.

When it's YOUR card, you read the back.

After a quick read, I wasn't sure what I had just read was really in print, so I read it a second time. I put the card down with a shake of my head. A third time read didn't produce any solace either. I pulled out the previous three cards from the Pirates, Tigers, and Yankees.

The back of the 2010 Pirates card reads, *Berger was a fantasy camp rookie and got a taste of the Championship as the Wagners, managed by Bill Virdon and Jerry Reuss, won their division and advanced to the Championship Game finishing with a 5–2 record. Berger batted .421, going eight for nineteen with seven RBIs and multiple aches and pains.*

Tigers 2011: *After a great rookie camp with Pittsburgh in 2010, Berger became a Tiger in 2011. He batted .667 with six hits in nine at-bats and six walks for an OBP of .800, helping lead a team coached by Frank Tanana and Darrell Evans to a 4–2 record in a rain-shortened camp. A career highlight, Berger defied the laws of aging and physics and chugged home on a sacrifice fly!*

Yankees 2012: *This is the third camp for Berger, having been with Pittsburgh in 2010 and Detroit in 2011. The Pinstripes, managed by Oscar Gamble and Homer Bush, started slow but closed strong, winning three of their last four to avoid the basement. Berger had a "career" game on January 19 on Steinbrenner Field with a 3-for-4 day, including his first extra base hit and a busy day with the glove. He also got drilled on the leg by an El Duque fastball!*

Nothing wrong with those. I'd be proud to pass them out at my next autograph show.

Then the 2013 card from the Pirates: *Berger returned to the Pirates after two years with the Tigers and Yankees. His defense helped the Traynors, led by Mike LaValliere and Don Robinson, win their division; but at age sixty, he slowed noticeably, batting .350 with six RBIs and stretched a triple into a double. He will probably retire.*

Retire? And never make that throw from first to third? Not a chance.

After all, it really is the most wonderful week of the year!

Finally on June 1, 2013, my first at-bat in a major league stadium at beautiful PNC Park.

Forty years later than I had planned but I finally get to play first base in
Pittsburgh as a Pirate.

Postgame

Epilogue

*M*y brother Mike and I cashed our Superstorm Sandy rain check and went to Yankees camp together one year later in November 2013. We had a week full of laughs and memories with the Yankees and 110 other pretend Yankees. It was a priceless experience that brought back the 1960s when we threw the ball in our backyard, but this time we were Doberman-free.

Fantasy camp is about making dreams come true. I still have one remaining. Mike puts his body back together and joins Jason, Scott, and me at Steinbrenner Field in Tampa to wear the pinstripes for a week. It's Saturday and the Legends game. David Wells returns to camp and is on the hill.

Mike leads off the inning by poking a line drive past Homer Bush at short, and thirty seconds later he finally lumbers safely to first. Jason, starting catcher on his 0–18 high school baseball team, tries to go opposite field and puts a ground ball just past the reach of Bucky Dent at second base, who thirty years ago easily turns that into a double play. Scott, a hockey player and high school boxer, walks to load the bases. It took two years, but I finally find another bat I like and head to the plate to face Wells. Somehow, I work the count full.

Boomer, wearing his Babe Ruth hat, grooves the payoff pitch, about 65 mph, right down the middle. I remember the Richie Hebner advice and swing as hard as I can, pivot, and make full contact with the ball. Yankees broadcaster John Sterling is in the radio booth. "There's a long drive...deep to right...it might be long enough...it could be..."

Damn. I hate that alarm clock.

Jason and Scott

Acknowledgments

*T*o my better half, Andi, for her love and support and insisting I live the dream.

To Jason and Scott for not thinking their dad is totally off his rocker and for keeping the Berger family baseball fire burning. We'll get on the field together one day soon.

To Herb Berger, for being the best dad of all-time, and for making me a Pirate early enough to remember the 1960 World Championship. Dad, this journey was for us.

To my mom, Arlene Berger, for keeping dinner warm so we could play one more inning. And even though you always made us wash our hands and change our clothes before we ate, we still love you.

To Fantasy Camp Directors Joe Billetdeaux, Julie Kremer, and Jerry Lewis: for running first-class operations and for tolerating me and all my questions. I thank you, and I want your job when I grow up.

To Peter Evans and Barry Otelsberg for putting yourselves at physical risk. Not many would have done it. Thanks for coming along and experiencing the thrill. You made our week very special.

To my coaches Bill Virdon, Jerry Reuss, Darrell Evans, Frank Tanana, Oscar Gamble, Homer Bush, Spanky LaValliere, and Don Robinson: a heartfelt thank-you for making me feel big-league.

To my lead inspiration team of Joe Allen and Lew Matusow along with Bill Apgar, Rich Balaban, Missy Betres, Kathy Carlson, Adam Cohen, Steve Dinkes, Robin Edinger, Heidi Evans, Eric Goldberg, Tim Lawler, Sidra and Dan Luciano, Dan Mitchell, David Moses, Dave Phillips, Howard Riech, Torme Santolli, Buzz Tabatchnick and countless others; friends from different walks of life whose daily camp encouragement got me out of bed each morning even if my legs begged me otherwise.

To the ad hoc photography team of Kate Gilbert, Barbara Kubala, Wendy Otelsberg, Jerry Otelsberg, Ruth Dmitrzak, Dan Heisserer, Doug Richey, and the Pirates, Tigers, and Yankees photo staffs: thanks for a camera that made an old guy look like he knew what he was doing.

To story editor Kate Kennedy and technical editor Greg Farley, my editing tandem and both huge BoSox fans: thanks for proving we can put Red Sox/Yankee hostility aside long enough to create a product to be proud of. And congratulations on your 2013 World Championship. If the Yankees ever get good again, we can go back to feuding.

To Andrea Kaye, Will McKee, and Jennifer Tidmore, thanks for your deft touch with copy, photos, and website.

To Mike Hallman for TheBat, which met a very untimely demise but more importantly for TheGlove, which is still treasured and going strong.

To Matthew McGough author of *Bat Boy* and to Larry Nickles who gifted it to me. It was the catalyst for this work.

To Gary Dworetz for his spot-on daily commentary and for suggesting a memoir. Hope it didn't disappoint.

To the BookLogix publishing team of Jessica Parker, Ellina Dent, Kelly Nightingale, and editor extraordinaire Caroline Donahue for coming in from the bullpen and pulling out a save for this rookie.

To Medjet Directors Harold Ripps, Wally Nall, Bob Reich, M. J. Hallman, Wally Nall III, Mat Whatley, and John Gobbels for your encouragement, patience, and for offering to have a medical jet parked near-by. That was one call I was happy not to make.

And finally, to Bill Mazeroski. As the baseball disappeared over the left field wall on October 13, 1960, and you rounded second base waving your helmet in the air with the World Championship secure, I ran outside my house and did the very same thing. That eight-year-old child could never have envisioned a time when I would ask you, and you would agree, to write the Foreword notes for my book. Fantasy meets reality indeed!

The required tools of a fantasy camp first baseman:
a dependable glove and a good tongue!

About the Author

*R*oy Berger is President and CEO of MedjetAssist, an air-medical transport membership company, based in Birmingham, Alabama. Prior to joining Medjet in 1998, Berger was in the pari-mutuel racing industry managing racetracks across the country, a career that ultimately spanned thirty-five years. Roy and his wife Andi live in Mountain Brook, Alabama. While Andi was born in  Detroit, other than wearing a Tigers jersey for this photo, she has no Detroit allegiance. In fact she prides herself a Pinstriper. They have two grown sons, Jason and Scott, whose careers have them living in Los Angeles and have distastefully become Dodgers fans. The house is ruled by Ibis, who halfway through the 2013 baseball season, thought it was pretty cool to be a Pirate and not just a chow/retriever mix.